SEX CHANGE

This book describes the post-operative adjustment of feminized transsexuals. It is a study in deviance management, rooted in interactionist theory and role theory.

Unlike the medical literature on transsexualism, this study does not focus on the etiology of the condition. It is a sociological study of the social relations of a group of transsexuals who have already undergone the sex change. The focus is on how the subjects get along post-operatively, what they do with their new lives as reborn women, what methods they use to achieve their sexual identity. Four types of adjustment have been identified: the housewife, the stripper, the aspiring housewife and the career woman. While these types differ primarily in terms of how much each values middle-class respectability, all transsexuals seem to subscribe to traditional conceptions of womanhood. The findings show that transsexuals are far more conservative and unliberated than randomly sampled normal males and females. Thus, the sex change is not only a step toward the achievement of female identity, but more importantly, toward the achievement of middle-class acceptance.

E

SEX CHANGE

The Achievement of Gender Identity Among Feminized Transsexuals

By

THOMAS KANDO

University of California
Riverside, California

CHARLES C THOMAS • PUBLISHER

Springfield • Illinois • U.S.A.

Published and Distributed Throughout the World by

CHARLES C THOMAS • PUBLISHER
Bannerstone House
301-327 East Lawrence Avenue, Springfield, Illinois, U.S.A.

©*1973, by* CHARLES C THOMAS • PUBLISHER

ISBN 0-398-02731-5

Library of Congress Catalog Card Number: 73-204

FOR ANITA

SEX CHANGE

While some transsexuals tend to appear as natural-born females more than others, (housewives, notably, more than strippers), all subjects use similar methods at one time or another.

For example, all lie, use accomplices, euphemisms, rationalizations, redefinitions of past biographical events, humor, voluntary stigma disclosure and withdrawal. Their effort throughout their interactions is at normalizing their relationships and constructing a coherent self-concept and identity. One paradox they must cope with is that they simultaneously try to account for their pathology, constructing psychoanalytic types of etiologies, but at the same time try to define themselves as natural females who were merely suffering from a minor biological aberration.

PREFACE

THIS book describes the post-operative adjustment of seventeen feminized transsexuals. The sex conversion operations took place as an experimental project at the University of Minnesota in 1967 and 1968. The patients were interviewed in 1968 and 1969, and so were some of their friends and relatives. The resulting data are primarily documentary, although some are quantitative, tentatively testing some hypotheses. Unlike the clinical literature on transsexualism, this study does not focus on the etiology of the condition. It is a sociological study of the social relations of transsexuals who have already undergone the sex change. The focus is on how the subjects get along now, what they do with their new lives as reborn women, what methods they use to achieve their sexual identity. While this book is a first in that it describes a population hitherto barely examined by sociologists, I hope that it offers more than merely a vignette of a specific category of deviance. The fluidity of contemporary sex roles is more than ever evident, as women's lib increasingly comes to mean liberation of both men and women; deviance and stigmatization are experienced by more and more people, as cultural pluralism and normative change become part of everyday life. It is to a better understanding of these important social problems that I hope to have made a contribution.

When it comes to acknowledging help and support, I cannot thank everyone who has contributed to the development and execution of this study, but a few deserve mention: Donald Hastings and Starke Hathaway, of the University of Minnesota Department of Psychiatry, who let me in on the project and gave me access to the respondents, and without whose invaluable cooperation this study would not have been possible; the sensitive and intelligent respondents themselves, whose enthusiastic cooperation stemmed from an eagerness to enable all of us to share in the exclusive knowledge which they have as a result of their unusual experience; Don Martindale, whose professional and moral help was as important for the realization of this project as it has been for contributions by dozens of other young sociologists; Laud Humphreys, Jim Powell, Jeff Hubbard and Jud Landis, who helped to improve this study methodologically and substantively; finally, Caroline Schaeffer and Lois Hill, whose secretarial work was really much more than just that.

T.K.

CONTENTS

Contents   xi

SEX CHANGE

Chapter 1

(INTRODUCTION)

COMMUTING to work in Minneapolis on a summer morning, I stopped to give a woman a ride. She claimed to have been standing at one of the city's major intersections for a considerable amount of time, trying in vain to hitch a ride. This surprised me, for she seemed too attractive to be in such a predicament very long. As I told her this, she paused for a moment and then said: "What would you say if I told you I'm a transsexual?" I replied that this would be inconceivable, laughing at what I believed to be a joke. She spent the remainder of the ride trying to convince me that she was indeed a transsexual and that several of her friends were likewise.

To this day I do not know whether Georgette, as I shall call her, was putting me on or not. She was a somewhat plump but quite attractive brunette of less than thirty, about whose gender there could be little doubt. Of course, my subsequent experience with a large number of feminized transsexuals taught me that many of these individuals are feminine to the point of being able to pass for natural-born females. Since I did not meet Georgette again when interviewing the transsexuals who underwent surgery at the University of Minnesota, she may, at best, have been a transvestite wishing for a sex-change operation.

Whatever the case may have been, this incident initiated me into the transsexual phenomenon. For Georgette not only awakened in me the desire to instigate a sociological inquiry into a rare phenomenon that had hitherto been only the topic of sick jokes and tabloid magazines, but she also introduced me to friends, some of whom were indeed transsexuals, others homosexuals or transvestites. Ultimately my research had to proceed through the formal channels of the University of Minnesota bureaucracy. Only thus was I able to gain access to and interview a maximum number

3

of feminized transsexuals. Nevertheless, the meeting with Georgette was fruitful. Having at first disbelieved her, I then accepted her invitation to be introduced to the subculture to which she belonged, an urban underworld subculture located in a number of gay bars, stripjoints and brothels, and whose membership included homosexuals, transvestites, transsexuals and professional female impersonators.

Up to my encounter with Georgette, my knowledge of transsexualism was limited to a vague acquaintance with the Christine Jorgensen case through newspapers and her just-published autobiography. I do not know whether Georgette's astounding confession, coming out of the blue and after we had barely met, caused me to react in an unusual manner. It may be that I would react differently now, after extensive contact with nearly twenty bona fide feminized transsexuals. In retrospect, while some of the transsexuals I subsequently interviewed were somewhat too odd to pass as natural-born females, others among them were attractive and as authentic in their feminine appearance as Georgette.

Thus, my experience with Georgette is illustrative of the central theme of this book: this was an encounter with an individual whose very sex was an issue. Georgette seemed to be a natural-born female; she claimed to be a transsexual; I disbelieved her, and had no immediate way of telling. It is this possibility of passing, resulting from the sex conversion and combined with the management of the new, female identity which typifies the social condition of all feminized transsexuals, whether they choose to pass or not. This encounter with Georgette was perhaps the best possible preparation for my subsequent study of bona fide feminized transsexuals. While none of these later respondents could play the same trick on me, for the simple reason that "they knew that I knew," it is eminently useful to have experienced the devastating psychological shock of suddenly not knowing the sex of one's interlocutor.

Transsexuals can be viewed as the first and only individuals who attempt to achieve the sex roles which, to other members of society, are ascribed by virtue of sex at birth. By undergoing a conversion operation, the transsexual in effect decides that sex at birth is no longer the insurmountable obstacle placed by nature between the individual and certain societal roles. In the transsexual's case, nature loses its ultimate primacy. Unlike the feminists who argue that the social structure is unjust with respect to women and therefore needs reform, transsexuals decide to alter their own physical sex in order to legitimately conform to cultural expectations.

Transsexuals, then, achieve a gender which others are born into. Subsequently as adults, they must laboriously learn to achieve the sex roles which others have had "naturally" ascribed to them from early childhood on. Transsexuals may therefore be expected to shed light on the processes involved in the acquisition of sex roles. While femininzed transsexuals may sometimes pass quite successfully as natural females, we know that they are not, and so do they. It is the transsexual's heightened awareness of the problems centering around the acquisition of sex roles and the enactment of culturally acceptable sex behavior that is tapped by the present study. These individuals can help us, for they are keenly sensitive to subtle cultural expectations which most of us take for granted to the point of not being aware of them.

Feminized transsexuals are a category of people who achieve a new gender identity and learn to play basic sex roles during their adult socialization. Their sex change represents a drastic status passage which may or may not entail passing. Transsexuals are knowledgeable, practical methodologists in the achievement of sex roles, the management of stigma-generated tensions in interaction and the management of information about their stigmatized identity. This is the transsexual's sociological position, and it is the product of their surgical feminization.

The physical feminization of a transsexual involves essentially the following phases: first a period of intensive psychological analysis, testing and counseling to determine the veracity of the subject's state of mind, his determination to go through the conversion, and his prospects for successful postoperative adjustment. The project on which the present study is based required a six-month preparatory phase of this kind, and it screened out felons and the mentally unstable. During the latter part of this phase, hormonal treatment begins, still a reversible process. The

patient is treated with estrogens, the female hormone, and
otherwise influenced in the reduction of his secondary male
characteristics and the development and reinforcement of female
characteristics. Much of the sex drive is lost and body hair is
reduced.

Once the patient has passed through these stages and is still
found determined to undergo the conversion operation, the
surgical phase takes place. This, then, consists of castration,
removal of the scrotum and the creation of an artificial vagina
entailing some skin transplant. The physical conversion is then
completed through silicone treatment which results in artificial
breasts, and electrolysis which removes facial hair. The transsexual's voice tends to remain low, but careful cultivation of this
aspect goes a long way toward concealing the former gender
altogether. In general, while feminized transsexuals tend to retain
a protruding Adam's apple, somewhat muscular features and a
number of other imperfections, the cultivation of feminine
etiquette, mannerism, attire and make-up results in truly
remarkable femininity. At worst, feminized transsexuals appear
somewhat odd. At best, they pass as authentic women. While no
transsexual can give birth to a child (ovary transplant is not yet a
scientific possibility), a majority of the subjects interviewed in this
book had enjoyed postoperative heterosexual intercourse, several
reporting vaginal orgasms. Three respondents were now married,
one to a man who did not know that his wife was a transsexual.
Among those who were not married but had had heterosexual
intercourse, several had, as prostitutes or otherwise, performed the
sex act with partners who did not know. Thus, many transsexuals
passed the test of the sex act itself, in their eyes the ultimate test
of womanhood.

In 1967, the University of Minnesota Hospital embarked on a
project that would, during the following two years, involve the
conversion operation of twenty-six transsexuals. A Gender
Identity Committee was created, consisting of Drs. Donald
Hastings of the Department of Psychiatry, Starke Hathaway of the
Department of Psychology, a surgeon and a number of other
members. The project was given some publicity, and hundreds of
applications of sex surgery were received, mostly from Minnesota,

some from other parts of the upper Midwest, over 90 percent from male transsexuals. The Identity Committee interviewed, tested and screened the applicants through the use of projective tests such as MMPI and known criminal records. The roughly two dozen applicants who were finally selected for the project were all male, all from Minnesota (necessitated by legal considerations) and ranging in age from twenty-one to well over fifty. In the eyes of the Committee, they were the most promising for successful postoperative adjustment. The conversion operations took place in 1968 and early 1969. Since then, a ten-year follow-up study has been under way to determine the patients' long-term adjustment as new females.

A majority of the patients are still in touch with the hospital. However, several have moved to such distant places as Hawaii, Canada, the West Coast and New Orleans. Some have no more been heard from, and some are rumored (through transsexuals still in contact with the hospital) to have lapsed into precarious situations, e.g. extreme hardship and social isolation coupled with prostitution and drugs, and second thoughts about the conversion operation. The majority of the patients are still in regular touch with the Gender Identity Committee. Their adjustment generally does not seem to be as precarious as the few rumored cases just mentioned; many are, in fact, quite elated about their new lives. A full report will be published at the conclusion of the follow-up study currently under way.

The present study is sociological. It was plugged into the University of Minnesota project in 1968. In cooperation with the Gender Identity Committee, I examined the patients' files, psychological tests results, biographical data and current addresses. By spring of 1969, when the last surgical operation had been completed, a letter was mailed to each subject, inviting her to return to the hospital for interviews about the social aspects of her sex conversion. Thus, I was able to talk, question and tape the content of several hours of interviews with a majority of these transsexuals. In addition, a structured questionnaire constructed prior to this phase was submitted to each respondent. Of those contacted by mail, twelve returned to the hospital for the requested interviews. Five were among those who had moved far

away, and they therefore only answered the structured questionnaire, which they returned by mail. The remaining transsexuals
were not available. Thus, the data reported in this study are
mostly based on seventeen cases, although contact was also made
with a couple of other transsexuals, appearing in Minneapolis
nightclubs but not part of the Minnesota project.

In addition to the open-ended interviews and the structured
questionnaires formally submitted and conducted in the hospital
offices, time was also spent in participant observation of the
Minneapolis homosexual-transvestite-transsexual subculture. A
number of gay bars, stripjoints and nightclubs were visited, first to
contact transsexuals known to circulate or to work there, later to
fraternize and observe the milieu. Furthermore, several transsexuals were visited at home and taken out socially. During this
process I became acquainted with some of the parents, siblings and
family conditions.

Finally, because some parts of the present study attempt to
show significant differences between the social relations of
transsexuals and those of natural-born males and females, the
structured questionnaire which was submitted to the converted
transsexuals was also mailed to a random sample of males and
females selected from the Minneapolis-Saint Paul metropolitan
area. These control groups were obtained by first randomly
sampling a large number of males and females from the city
directories and then selecting from these samples a group of
seventeen males and a group of seventeen females whose distribu-
tions matched those of the transsexuals as closely as possible along
seven crucial control variables, namely age, education, marital
status, religion, socioeconomic status, birthplace and size of
birthplace. Thus, some quantitative analyses were performed,
comparing seventeen transsexuals with equal numbers of males
and females used as control groups.

The central focus of all portions of the study, regardless of the
methodology used, is on the transsexual's postoperative social
relationships. The etiological issue, amply dealt with in the
medical literature (Benjamin, 1964, 1966; Green and Money,
1969; Hamburger, 1953; Walinder, 1967) and in the psychological-
psychiatric literature (Green and Money, 1969; Pauly, 1965;

Stoller, 1968; Worden, 1955), is not what this study sets out to examine. Rather, the study begins with the postoperative examination of transsexuals and asks: How do these individuals handle their social relations *from here on?* How do they learn and react to new role expectations; what practical methods do they develop to handle their stigma, be it known or covert; do they attempt to pass or not, and why? In sum, how does the converted transsexual succeed as a social person?

SOME TYPICAL CASES

In terms of overall femininity in appearance, the respondents ranged from odd to near perfection. Sally was the first patient to undergo surgery at the University of Minnesota. This had occurred nearly two years prior to our first interview, which took place in a university office. Sally was a tall and slender blonde of twenty-eight, who wore her long hair loose and dressed in an attractive miniskirt revealing legs only slightly on the muscular side. She arrived nearly one hour late for our first interview, apologizing profusely but cheerfully chatting with secretaries and hospital personnel. Her voice was high, her mannerisms seductive. Sitting cross-legged and blowing out cigarette smoke in typical girlish fashion seemed by now second nature to her. She was now married and appeared quite elated about her new life. Only once during our first interview did she become somber. This occurred when she related how her family had "disowned" and repudiated her since the conversion operation. She came from a rural, upper-Midwestern environment. Her family was protestant. Her father, a retired farmer, wanted nothing to do with her now. Allegedly her family did not want her to visit home. Yet Sally expressed little bitterness. She soon pulled herself out of these depressing contemplations and dismissed her family's attitude with the words "they are just plain, ignorant people."

Much more important to her were the various attractions of her new life as a woman. When asked to elaborate upon her married life she confessed, again somewhat pensively and with girlish shyness, that her husband did not know that she was a sex change. However, she soon dismissed this problem from her mind, too. She preferred to discuss, jovially, anecdotes about the new pleasures of being a housewife. Talking about her husband, she said: "I really love him. He is so gentle and so good to me. . . . He is a real hard worker too; he is going back to night school soon. . . . He has gained forty pounds since we got married; he must like my cooking!" At first glance, then, Sally seemed to be highly successful in her adjustment, highly feminine and a testimony to the possibility of successful gender passage.

Equally feminine, but in a darker, more mysterious way, was Elizabeth, a tall, beautiful blonde woman of twenty-eight. During our first interview she seemed somewhat sad. She was very well dressed, her hairdo and facial make-up were meticulous. She told how much she was in love with her present boyfriend, who was still married but had promised to get a divorce and marry her. Would this relationship fail, Elizabeth warned that she would not have the strength to go on living. In fact, she said that she had already attempted suicide a few months earlier, when he had threatened to leave her. Such allusions to suicide highlighted her general melancholy. Besides her problematic love affair with a married man, Elizabeth's sex surgery had been less than satisfactory. She had had to return to the hospital for corrective surgery several times since the initial operation, nearly 1 1/2 years ago, and still she said that she had "not been able to function as a woman, yet."

Coming from a small Minnesota town where her father was a craftsman, having been raised in a Lutheran family and school environment, Elizabeth now appeared to be a highly sophisticated woman of the world. She admitted to earning a great deal of money as a highbrow Minneapolis hairdresser. In general, she appeared to be another case of an eminently successful sex reassignment insofar as first-glance identification is concerned. While temperamentally, she may not have been the happy-go-lucky housewife that Sally had become, she was a profoundly attractive woman who could become very successful professionally and otherwise.

Linda, too, had become a very attractive young woman. I first interviewed her in a downtown nightclub where she performed as a stage dancer and stripper. At that time, Linda was twenty-eight.

Her black hair and dark complexion suggested a Latin ethnic origin. Nevertheless, she also came from a protestant, rural Minnesota environment.

The interview took place at a back table of the nightclub, during intermission. I purchased two drinks and from all visible appearances I simply may have been "on the make" with one of the stage girls. Indeed, Linda's bodily features, considerably exposed under the circumstances, were exquisitely feminine. So was her behavior. While prior to her operation she had cross-dressed for many years and appeared in various nightclubs as a female impersonator, her present show did *not* feature her as a sex change. In other words, her sex reassignment was so successful that she had been able, at least professionally, to pass as a natural-born female.

Indeed, she explained that her conversion, which occurred nearly two years prior to this interview, was immediately successful, both surgically and cosmetically. Unlike most other patients, Linda did not have to return to the hospital for corrective surgery. Convalescence took only nine days, at the end of which she went home a full-fledged woman. She had had no difficulty experiencing vaginal orgasm.

In a sense, Linda may have been the best adjusted female of the entire group. By this I mean the fact that to her, unlike most other transsexuals, the whole issue of transsexualism had begun to be a bore. She did not seem interested in discussing her condition and her sex change. What is more, this did not appear to result from defensiveness, but genuine boredom with the subject. "Thank God that's over," she said. She seemed to have transcended that momentous episode in her life, wanting now only to forget it and live the life of a woman.

Thus, she seemed somewhat impatient with my naive questioning, becoming more talkative and friendly when the conversation moved to areas unrelated to transsexualism. When asked how she felt about public disclosure of her sex change, and what she thought of other transsexuals, she replied: "I don't care, it's over now. . . . I don't socialize with other transsexuals, all my friends are now heteros. . . ." She was thus rejecting roles of patient, curiosity, freak or object of scientific inquiry. The fact that she may have been more interested in me as a prospective date than a sociologist may have been the healthiest sign of all. It goes without saying that she was able to develop these attitudes only because of the very successful nature of her physiological change.

Sally, Elizabeth, Linda and Maryjo were all attractive and highly feminine examples of very successful sex reassignment. At the opposite end of the spectrum were Lisa and Roberta. Members of the hospital staff briefed me about Lisa before I interviewed her. I had been told that she was an older, very large, loud and bombastic transsexual, quite different from most other patients. Her first appearance in my office was indeed in style: well over six feet tall, fifty years old, weighing probably more than two hundred pounds, she was accompanied by an entourage that included her boyfriend, a shy and slender young man about half her size. Lisa's dyed hair was arranged in a fancy chignon further accentuating her size. She wore a miniskirt that revealed powerful athletic legs and gave her overall appearance a sense of something grotesque. When she arrived, she was talking cheerfully to everyone around, greeting various people in her baritone voice, finally peeking into my office and saying: "Hi honey, I'll be there in a moment."

Lisa had been born in Chicago. She was the only Jew in the sample. She had worked much of her life as a female impersonator in various parts of the country. As a male before the operation, she claimed to have been married three times without sexual consumation of any of her short-lived marriages. Since her operation she had been employed as a nightclub singer in Canada. It is inconceivable that Lisa would have attempted to perform as a bona fide female. Yet she claimed that "up in Canada, nobody knows." Whatever the case may be, her sex reassignment had an entirely different meaning than that of cases discussed earlier: there was no hope for her to pass as a natural-born female.

Sexually, her operation had been problematic. In her own words: "I stayed at the hospital for two months; I was very sick, I had complications, urine problems. They don't want me to come back for corrective surgery because I'm too old. Now I have everything but it doesn't work. I have lost my sex drive anyway,

I'm too afraid." While Lisa was quite happy about her sex change, never expressing regrets or second thoughts, she did not expect the same total fulfillment as a female, including marital domesticity and status passage, as did most of her younger fellow patients. While her situation may have been termed satisfactory since her expectations were realistic, her feminization left a great deal to be desired.

Roberta was also much older than the average transsexual at the time of her sex conversion. She may have been the most problematic case in the sample. I interviewed her at home, only four weeks after her release from the hospital. She was still in bed. The ravages of the surgical and hormonal intervention were very evident. Her complexion was rough and unshaven, her hair short, uneven, messy. She claimed to be fifty-one but seemed older. Our interviews were longer and deeper than those with other transsexuals, possibly because Roberta, a college graduate and business executive, was more lucid, verbal, objective and analytical about her situation than other transsexuals.

Unlike other patients, she had lived through one, long, conventional marriage during which she had fathered a girl now twenty years old. She had occasionally cross-dressed, a habit tolerated by her former wife and unknown to her daughter. She had never been a homosexual, had no contacts with the transvestite-transsexual subculture, in sum, she did not follow the general pattern that culminates in sex change. When she had obtained her divorce from her wife a year and a half ago, no one expected her to become a transsexual. Yet her plans to go through with the operation, she maintained, went back many years, taking shape gradually as she had become increasingly disenchanted and burdened by her marriage. Roberta now expected to go back to the same executive position with the same firm as before the operation. In her own words:

> I don't know what is going to happen, because I've only worked as a male. It will be interesting to see what is going to happen . . . I don't fear going back, I welcome the idea. I think it will be terribly interesting just as a sociological study to see how I will be accepted. I'm just dying to go back. I have a large office, there are thirty people in the office that work for me and it would be quite interesting to

know how many people are going to say 'I don't want to work in this
nut house,' or how many people will accept. I'll advise my employer
before I go back and the circumstances. I hope to get the help of a
psychiatrist to discuss this with him. We have a psychologist on the
payroll, I expect to talk to him beforehand.

Apart from the unreality of this expectation, what may have
turned out to be Roberta's greatest problem was her appearance.
Having changed sex at such an old age and having led the life of a
seemingly well-adjusted male, the first postoperative impression
she made on me was simply that of a man, an intelligent, lucid and
physically sick man. Roberta's voice was low; her speech patterns,
vocabulary and appearance were masculine. Some of this may in
time be remedied, but at that point she appeared to be the worst
case of sex reassignment of the entire sample.

Thus, at first glance, some feminized transsexuals seemed to
have undergone a very successful sex change, some less so, and in
some cases it was difficult to visualize how they would surmount
the barriers that still separated them from any semblance of
womanhood. Three things emerged at the very outset: young
transsexuals were always more successfully feminized than older
ones; the more time which had lapsed since the conversion
operation, the more feminine and better adjusted the subjects
seemed to be; those transsexuals who had cross-dressed extensively
and for long periods of time prior to their operation seemed more
fully feminized than those who had not.

In the next chapter, the boundaries of the study are further
delineated, both in terms of the issues dealt with and the methods
employed. The focus of the study will be on the various patterns
of postoperative adjustment, and the method is primarily
descriptive ethnographic. Several contrasting patterns of adjustment are revealed: one type, that of the transsexual who seeks to
marry, settle down, establish middle-class respectability and
passage as a natural female, has been labeled the "housewife
type." At the opposite extreme are the transsexuals who opt for a
show business career, as did Christine Jorgensen, advertising and
exploiting their sex change. This pattern has been called the
"Christine Jorgensen model," or the "showbusiness pattern." The
housewife type, the showbusiness type and intermediate types of

adjustment are examined and contrasted. Each type's motives, goals and attitudes are documented and discussed. All transsexuals are examined in terms of their attitudes towards sex roles, masculinity, femininity, their gender self-concept, their sex definitions and the sex role strains which they experience.

In Chapter 3, verbatim case material from the interviews is presented to illustrate each of four postoperative types of adjustment.

Chapters 4 and 5 link the typology that has been established to a sociological theory of stigma management. All transsexuals bear stigma and all are faced with the basic question: to pass or not to pass? All reveal and acknowledge their stigma in some situations, and all try to conceal it in other situations, even though the housewife type opts more frequently for the latter strategy than the show business type. The different types enable us to make some generalizations about how stigmatized individuals manage information about their identity, and how they manage tension in interaction.

Finally, in the concluding chapter, the theoretical implications of a study of transsexuals and other stigmatized individuals are further delineated. The transsexual, it is pointed out, is particularly useful for our understanding of adult socialization into basic sex roles and the practical methodology involved in the achievement of proper sex behavior. In addition, transsexuals exhibit many methods of stigma management in general. Therefore, transsexuals represent a population of strategic importance for those interested in the social psychology of sex and gender.

REFERENCES

Benjamin, Harry: Nature and management of transsexualism, with a report on 31 operated cases. Western Journal of Surgery, Obstetrics and Gynecology, 72:105-111, 1964.
––– The Transsexual Phenomenon. New York, Julian Press, 1966.
Driscoll, James P.: Transsexuals. Transaction (March-April). Special Supplement. PP. 28-37, 66, 68; 1971.
Edwards, John N.: The Family and Change.
Ellis, Albert: The Folklore of Sex. New York, Grove Press, 1961.
Garfinkel, Harold: Studies in Ethnomethodology. Englewood Cliffs, N.J., Prentice-Hall, 1967, pp. 116-185.

Goffman, Erving: Stigma: Notes on the Management of Spoiled Identity. Englewood Cliffs, N.J., Prentice-Hall, 1963.

Green, Richard, and Money, John: Transsexualism and Sex Reassignment. Baltimore, The Johns Hopkins Press, 1969.

Hamburger, Christian; Sturup, George K., and Dahl-Iverson, E.: Transvestism: Hormonal, psychiatric and surgical treatment. JAMA, 152:391-396, 1953.

Hunt, Morton: The future of marriage. Playboy, 18:116, 1971.

Jorgensen, Christine: A Personal Autobiography. New York, Bantam Books, 1968.

Kinsey, A. C.; Pomeroy, W. B., and Martin, C. E.: Sexual Behavior in the Human Male. Philadelphia, Saunders, 1948.

Linton, Ralph: The Study of Man: An Introduction. New York, Appleton-Century-Crofts, 1936.

Pauly, Ira B.: Male psychosexual inversion: Transsexualism. Arch Gen Psychiatry, 13:172-181, 1965.

Stoller, Robert J.: Sex and Gender: On the Development of Masculinity and Femininity. New York, Science House, 1968.

Walinder, J.: Transsexualism: A Study of Forty-three Cases. Goteborg, Scandinavian University Books, 1967.

Worden, Frederick G., and Marsh, James T.: Psychological factors in men seeking sex transformation. JAMA, 157:1292-1298, 1955.

Chapter 2

(SOLVING AN)
IDENTITY CONFLICT

TRANSSEXUALISM can be described as an identity conflict between mind and body. Therefore, the conflict can be resolved by (a) adapting the mind to the body or (b) adapting the body to the mind, i.e. through psychotherapy, or surgical and endocrinological treatment.

It is generally agreed that psychotherapy has failed to cure transsexualism. The nonsurgical management of these problems simply does not work. According to Benjamin, "that transvestites can simply use willpower and stop 'dressing' is nonsense." Neither has behavior modification achieved any significant results towards the cure of transvestites and transsexuals. Thus, conversion operation remains the main solution. For a fee ranging from $2,000 to $4,000, a patient can get the entire operation, which consists of castration, penectomy, plastic surgery and the creation of an artificial vagina, as well as preparatory hormonal treatment. Benjamin's estimate of the results, based on a sample of fifty-one male transsexuals between the ages of twenty and fifty-eight, is as follows:

33 percent good,

53 percent satisfactory,

4 percent unsatisfactory.

As far as female transsexuals are concerned (these account for about one fourth of all transsexuals), most conversions in this direction are quite successful from both the biological and the psychological standpoints.

The psychiatrist Stoller is more skeptical of surgery than Benjamin. He points to the high frequency of prostitution, exhibitionism and other symptoms of maladjustment among transsexuals postoperatively. According to Stoller, *if* a psychiatrist is to recommend a patient for surgery, this should occur only after the most elaborate screening process. Benjamin has devised a method of evaluation and treatment which can be usefully applied: after weeding out those patients who obviously are psychologically unsuited, he suggests to his candidates that they actually pass as women for many months. He has found that for some, while the phantasies of being a woman are very rich, the rigors of living as a woman are either too frightening or the person is too masculine to be able to keep it up. During this time, Benjamin prescribes estrogens, believing that they not only give the patient an inner sense of femaleness and an observable change in body contours, but that the estrogens in themselves have a tranquilizing effect on males. If after this trial the patient, in the doctor's opinion, is still highly motivated and sufficiently feminine, he is then referred to surgery. After this has taken place, the patients should be followed up indefinitely.

In conclusion, Stoller agrees with Benjamin that "we have to come to terms with the problem. We cannot legislate it away, probably, and we do not know how to treat it psychiatrically." However, the author's acknowledgement that gender identity cannot shift easily does not imply that he feels that surgery is the only solution: transsexualism is reversible in childhood, and this is where Stoller sees a task for psychotherapy.

In sum, there are those who believe that transsexualism is inborn, and those who believe that it is learned. While the issue has not yet been settled, current evidence is in favor of the latter position. Nevertheless, everyone concurs that the condition is not curable through psychotherapy or any other form of psychological conditioning, because it is too deeply engrained in the subjects, probably as a result of very early childhood socialization.

One of the first objectives of this study was to establish some significant characteristics of transsexuals per se. It was desirable to compare the seventeen feminized transsexuals with a number of normal males and females selected randomly from the general population, in order to determine some of the social and psychological features which separate transsexuals from non-transsexuals, and which unite transsexuals as a sociological category. Therefore, a sample of men and women was drawn randomly from the Minneapolis-Saint Paul metropolitan area, the area in which most transsexuals lived. In order to focus on important social-psychological differences between transsexuals and nontranssexuals, a number of variables had to be controlled. Therefore a subsample was obtained, matching the transsexuals as closely as possible along seven basic demographic variables: age, marital status, birthplace, education, religion, socioeconomic status and size of birthplace. Table I presents the distribution of the seventeen transsexuals and equal numbers of males and females used for comparative purposes along these variables. All respondents were white.

It was decided to compare males, females and transsexuals in five major areas: overall masculinity and femininity, attitudes towards current definitions of masculinity and femininity, role strain, definitions of sex and gender, and attitudes towards transsexualism.

Masculinity-Femininity

We call behavior and attitudes masculine or feminine when they are in accord with cultural definitions of proper male or female roles, styles and attitudes. In this sense, most men learn to become masculine and most women learn to become feminine. A masculine woman is one who does not conform to the cultural stereotype, and so is a feminine man. While there is overlap, some women being more masculine than some men and some men being more feminine than some women, masculinity-femininity tests show that men are generally more masculine than women. These tests do not measure the inherent nature of things, but merely that the majority of men and women behave as our culture wants them to.

Existing masculinity-femininity scales measure masculinity and femininity through a number of items that deal with tastes, habits, preferences, attitudes and roles. Many of these scales are indirect in the sense that they use statements which have an unapparent relationship to masculinity or femininity. Through repeated use over many years, these scales have proved that they discriminate

Sex Change

Table I

DISTRIBUTION OF TRANSSEXUALS, MALES AND
FEMALES, ALONG SEVEN CONTROL VARIABLES*

Variable	Transsexuals	Males	Females
Age			
22 and younger	0	0	1
22-25	2	1	2
26-35	10	9	9
36-43	2	0	2
44 and over	2	7	3
No information	1	0	0
Marital Status			
Married	4	14	11
Single	10	3	4
Divorced, separated, widowed	3	0	2
Birthplace			
Midwest	12	15	14
East	1	1	2
South	0	1	1
Foreign	2	0	0
No information	2	0	0
Education			
Completed grammar school	3	2	0
Completed high school	9	4	13
Some college	2	7	3
Completed college	2	4	1
No information	1	0	0
Religion			
Protestant	9	9	11
Roman Catholic	6	5	5
Jewish	1	1	1
No preference	1	2	0
Socioeconomic Status			
Father professional	1	0	1
Father proprietor, manager or farmer	4	6	6
Father craftsman	5	6	4
Father operative	3	0	1
Father salesman	2	2	1
Father laborer	2	2	4
Father in services	0	1	0

Variable	Transsexuals	Males	Females
Size of Birthplace			
Rural and small town (under 10,000)	10	8	9
Middle-sized city (10,000-100,000)	2	0	2
Large city (100,000-500,000)	0	5	2
Metropolis (over 500,000)	5	4	4

*The matching in this table is an approximation of transsexuals by males and females when considering seven variables *simultaneously,* as the computer was programmed for. In addition, the computer was instructed to *weigh* some variables more heavily than others, for example education twice as heavily as religion. What this means, commonsensically, is that we did not go as much out of our way to match the samples in terms of religion, as we did for education. Nevertheless, some variables turned out to be very difficult to match. For example, probably as a result of the selective response to our mailed questionnaire (less than a 20% response rate in spite of two rounds of questioning), hardly any single people were to be found among the hundreds of returned questionnaires. Hence, the serious imperfections in the matching in Table I.

between men and women, or at least between masculine and feminine individuals. They possess, in one word, face validity. However, it is not exactly clear what these scales measure over and beyond the vague psychological entity "masculinity" which individuals supposedly possess to a greater or lesser extent.*

Here, the question was a simple one: how do transsexuals, males and females compare with one another when it comes to possessing features deemed masculine or feminine by our culture, particularly roles and attitudes? That men and women differ significantly is evident. But what about transsexuals? Do they constitute a distinct category in this respect, and if so, are they more feminine than men only, or more feminine than both men and women?

In order to answer these questions, a masculinity-femininity scale was constructed to cover the five cultural areas in which differences were most likely to exist: attitudes, skills and responsibilities, occupational roles, other roles, and gender attributes. For each of these areas many items were derived from the pertinent literature and pretested. Finally, twenty-six items

*For a discussion of various masculinity-femininity scales, including the MMPI and the Marke-Gottfries scales, see Walinder (1967).

were retained. The resulting scale turned out to be highly valid and reliable in the sense that it discriminates very consistently between men and women. One item out of each of the scale's five sub-areas has been reproduced below:

I (would) love to have children.

I am the primary supporter of my family.

My occupation is . . . .

In general, I (would) submit to my husband's (wife's) decisions.

Engagement and wedding rings are very important to me.

The three gender groups were given an identical questionnaire that included the masculinity-femininity scale. A Kruskal-Wallis one-way analysis of variance was performed to test the significance of the differences between the average scores of males, females and transsexuals.* A statistic value of 25.06 was obtained, which is significant beyond the .001 level. As expected, males scored the highest, i.e. the most masculine. Unexpectedly, however, transsexuals scored significantly lower than both males and females. Thus, according to the scale used in this study, transsexuals were found to be the most feminine group, in terms of selected attitudes, skills and responsibilities, occupations, certain roles, and some gender attributes. While no claim is being made at this point to assert that transsexuals are fundamentally and psychologically more feminine than both men and women, the test nevertheless shows that they are, in many of their everyday activities, attitudes, habits and emphases what our culture expects women to be, only more so.

Attitudes Towards Cultural Definitions of Masculinity and Femininity

A second way is which transsexuals could be expected to differ

---

*The Kruskal-Wallis one-way analysis of variance by ranks is a non-parametric test for the differences between the rank-ordering of three or more groups. Since the transsexuals were not selected randomly from a population, and since the M-F scores represent ordinal data, a test had to be selected that makes no assumptions about the data or a population that they might represent. Since the object of the test was to show that the variation between the groups (males, females and transsexuals) is significantly larger than that *within* each group, an analysis of variance was called for. Since the M-F scores of the respondents were ranked, a test of rank differences was needed. As a non-parametric analysis of variance by ranks, the Kruskal-Wallis test was therefore selected. For further information about this test, see Siegel (1956).

from males and females is the extent to which they *endorse* our society's dominant sex and gender norms. While it is clear that women are in growing disagreement with men about the way society ascribes roles, responsibilities and attitudes to each sex, transsexuals could also be expected to disagree, albeit in a different fashion. While women today demand full equality in such areas as occupations, thus wishing to masculinize some of their roles, transsexuals are individuals who have been unable to play the masculine roles ascribed to them by society, ending up feminizing themselves.

In order to compare the three gender groups in this respect, a second scale was constructed, consisting of items that parallel those of the M-F (masculinity-femininity) scale. For each M-F item, a corresponding normative statement was formulated to measure the extent of each respondent's agreement with traditional sex ascriptions. In Table II, five M-F items have been reproduced, along with their normative counterparts.

Males, females and transsexuals were asked the extent of their agreement or disagreement with each normative statement, and a Kruskal-Wallis test was used to evaluate the significance of the

Table II

MASCULINITY-FEMININITY ITEMS, AND THEIR NORMATIVE
COUNTERPARTS USED TO MEASURE SEXUAL CONSERVATISM

M-F Statements	Normative Statements
I (would) love to have children.	Women must have a greater desire to have children than do men.
I am the primary supporter of my family.	A husband's primary responsibility is to support his family, while a wife's primary responsibility is to design the way of life of the family.
My occupation is	It is proper that most . . . should be men (resp. women).
In general, I (would) submit to my husband's (wife's) decisions.	Ultimately, a woman should submit to her husband's decisions.
Engagement and wedding rings are very important to me.	Engagement and wedding rings must be more important to women than to men.

observed differences. A statistic of 11.55 was obtained, significant beyond the .01 level. As expected, men were in overwhelmingly greater agreement than women with the cultural sex ascriptions tapped by the scale. Furthermore, transsexuals once again turned out to score more extremely than either males or females. In this case, however, unlike with the M-F scale, the transsexuals' scores were the highest, not the lowest. This suggests that these individuals are more conservative in their support of traditional sex role ascriptions than males and females.

Role Strain

A third area in which transsexuals could be expected to differ from other respondents is that of role strain in regard to sex roles, i.e. conflict between the sex roles one is expected to play in society and the roles one is most willing and best able to play (Goode, 1960).

The findings obtained by the two scales bear on this matter: The scales showed men to be the most masculine group, and also to willingly accept current definitions of masculinity-femininity. Hence, men can be said to experience little role strain in this area. Women, on the other hand, were shown to be feminine, but to reject current definitions of proper masculinity-femininity. Our female respondents thereby expressed a conflict between wish and reality with respect to sex roles. Transsexuals, finally, had highly feminine scores on the M-F scale and highly conservative scores on the normative scale. These conservative scores indicate that transsexuals willingly accept traditional norms of femininity. Hence transsexuals, like males, experience little role strain with respect to sex roles. The argument is summarized in Table III.

That transsexuals rigorouly accept cultural sex ascriptions may be documented from the case material. Their highly conservative views regarding proper sex roles were evidenced in almost every interview. Elinor, for example, said: "The ultimate criterion of being a woman is being a good wife, being able to make a man happy."

Elizabeth expressed similar feelings when she said: "I feel that

Table III

	Normative scale indicates that:		M-F scale indicates that:	Hence:
Males	accept cultural ascriptions of masculinity	and	possess masculine roles and characteristics	experience little strain
Females	reject cultural ascriptions of feminity	and	possess, in fact, feminine roles and characteristics	experience strain
Trans- sexuals	accept cultural ascriptions of femininity	and	possess feminine roles and characteristics	experience little strain

everything should be distinctly masculine or feminine. My boy friend has to look like a real man. . . . I'm opposed to those unisex clothes they're selling in New York. . . ."

And Jane added, with equal zeal: "Woman has no business being in business, unless there is something wrong with her. . . . Men should be the leaders."

And finally Maryjo, when asked whether women should get equal pay with men, answers: "Not at all! I feel that a man should make more than a woman!"

Similarly, the fact that transsexuals also possess feminine roles and characteristics is quite clear from the case material. For example, Sally has already been quoted as saying "I'm now a fulltime housewife. . . . He has gained forty pounds since we got married, he must like my cooking. . . ." Most significantly, Sally's husband does not *know,* which indicates that she has passed so effectively as a natural-born female that not even the sex act betrays her true identity.

Among the seventeen feminized transsexuals interviewed, several (proudly) proclaimed to be housewives and nothing but housewives. In addition, those who worked had the following jobs: secretaries (3), waitress (1), dancers (4), hairdressers or beauticians (2), actresses (2), university-affiliated research scientist (1).

While the transsexuals' femininity in the other areas measured by the scale is more difficult to demonstrate, since all we have to go by are the subjects' own statements, it is nevertheless clear that their responses to the M-F scale were generally more than mere wishful thinking. It became clear from the responses as well as from observation and increasing personal acquaintance with the transsexuals that their roles and skills in various areas were indeed generally those of women, only often more so.

Ultimately the best proof of the fact that many transsexuals have achieved a high degree of femininity is that several of them pass as natural-born females in an increasing number of situations. For example, in addition to Sally, three other transsexuals are now married; several work as strippers in nightclubs; those with more "respectable" jobs interact daily with clients, colleagues and superiors, most of whom do not know. These facts attest to the transsexuals' femininity.

Thus it is logical that transsexuals do not express the same discontent with their roles as women. How they feel about the strain of sex role obligations is probably best summarized in Sylvia's words: "Before, I felt like a woman and if I behaved like a woman it was noticeable and nonacceptable, whereas now it's acceptable. In fact, a woman can behave in almost any way and it's acceptable, I mean respectable. There isn't as much emphasis put on how a woman acts as there is on how a man acts. . . . A man must act slightly masculine. If a woman acts masculine, people don't notice it as much as they do when a man acts feminine.

What this indicates is that to Sylvia, as to most transsexuals, feminization has produced strain reduction. Certainly tensions remain in the transsexual's postoperative life, but these result primarily from the fact that she must either pass and manage information about herself, or acknowledge her stigma and manage tension in interaction. In any event, the surgical conversion operation facilitates and legitimizes playing the desired and achievable sex roles, i.e. it is a strategy in strain reduction. Women were inferred to experience the greatest role strain of any gender group, a strain they would reduce by moving in a direction opposite to the transsexuals, i.e. by masculinizing some of their roles if given the opportunity. To the strain caused by cultural definitions of sex roles, transsexuals have found a solution that makes them, in this respect, better adjusted than females.

Sex Definitions and Gender Identity

Sex is not merely biologically determined; it is also socially defined. While this is an academic point for normal males and females, transsexuals are keenly aware of this since they opt for a social definition of their gender that clashes with nature. Transsexuals firmly believe that they are real women, and that they have been real women all along.

Feminized transsexuals have acquired vaginas, but they do not possess all of a woman's features. The primary "imperfection" is their inability to bear children. What then, are the criteria used by transsexuals to define sex and gender in such a way that they may qualify as genuine women? Surely transsexuals, females and possibly males will each emphasize different criteria when it comes to defining sex and gender.

To test this hypothesis, all respondents were asked what they consider to be the ultimate criterion of being a woman. The question was open-ended and it produced multiple answers, thus making coding undesirable. Nevertheless, the following patterns could be discerned: The majority of males emphasized biological criteria (13 out of 17), while failing to discriminate strongly between vagina and reproductive organs. Women, on the other hand, emphasized social-psychological criteria (11 out of 17 mentioned "behaving like a woman"). Insofar as women mentioned biological criteria, they specified reproductive organs (4 subjects). Transsexuals, finally, emphasized mostly social-psychological criteria (10 out of 17 mentioned such things as "being attracted to men," being loved and needed by the family" and "behaving like a woman"), but some also used a biological criterion, and those that did emphasized, understandably, possession of a vagina (5 subjects).

These findings may be evidence of something quite interesting: feminized transsexuals, as we know, are by no means generally accepted as real women. However, they undoubtedly define themselves as real women. Therefore, when asked what they

consider to be the ultimate criterion of being a woman, the
following types of answers were given:

Elinor: It's feeling like a woman. It is possible to be physically a
man and yet truly a woman. It is one's personality, mind, outlook,
that make the difference. I had three homosexual affairs before the
operation. They were all unsuccessful . . . I despised them. To me
these affairs were not homosexual. They were one-sided. I played a
passive role. I derived no pleasure from them. I felt I was a
woman. . . .

Elizabeth: . . . behaving like a woman, since I can't have sex and I
can't have children . . . What I'd like most is to have a child, but I
couldn't.

Adelaide: I can't answer that. It would be better to ask what is the
ultimate goal. I was always a woman, I wasn't a man. I tried terribly
hard to conform to male roles, I tried to survive. I dressed well and
neatly, I never cross-dressed, I tried to express the difference between
a woman and a man in my appearance. But Donald looked like a nelly
boy.

Linda: Having a vagina. There are lots of masculine women, but
this doesn't make them males. Being able to bear children is not what
makes the difference either: look at all the women with hysterectomy. I can love my children as much as if I'd gone through
childbirth. My greatest ambition is to be a mother before I'm thirty,
through adoption of course.

It appears that in every instance the transsexual's criterion of
real womanhood is one by which she qualifies. Furthermore, the
responses of males and females indicate that each gender group,
not only transsexuals, uses sex definitions that are best suited to
its own purposes. To men, it is sufficient to define womanhood in
broad biological terms. Our female respondents, however, knowing
the context in which they were asked to answer the question, had
to emphasize that biological criterion according to which *only*
natural-born females qualify, namely ovaries. Thus, while sex
definitions are not generally explicit in our awareness, while we all
"know a man, or a woman, when we see one" and generally leave
it at that, the use of transsexuals here has shown one ethnomethodology which most of us probably use unwittingly, namely
to use that sex definition which will enable us most unequivocally
to classify ourselves in the desired gender group.

Attitudes Towards Transsexualism

With regard to the transsexuals' ultimate gender in the eyes of others, one question asked of all normals was: "Do you feel that transsexuals who have successfully undergone the conversion operation are now real women?" Only five respondents (2 women, 3 men) agreed that such feminized transsexuals may now be considered real women. Most respondents did not agree, and in addition they offered various alternative therapeutic suggestions. For example, a twenty-eight-year-old university coed felt that "... more study should be done with these people emotionally before the operation, otherwise I feel it is a good thing for people with this serious identification problem."

A twenty-six-year-old housewife said: "They are biologically different, i.e. they cannot bear children, *etc.* . . . I feel that sex change operations are only a physical way of trying to help when really there is something wrong psychologically. I feel sorry for transsexuals as I feel what they are is not their own fault. It's too bad that parents of transsexuals could not have the psychiatric help *they* need *before* they're allowed to have children."

Finally, some respondents could simply not accept the fact of transsexualism. For example, a fifty-year-old engineer, with some college and a rural background, said: "I think this was the most stupid study I've ever been involved with. Must be someone with a warped mind to be able to think this up just to analyze people. . . ."

Thus, whether a person's attitudes towards transsexuals are benevolent or not, the overwhelming feeling is that they are not real women.

In addition, we had access to data showing how some men and some women feel about certain aspects of transsexualism. Hathaway had asked about two hundred respondents a number of questions about this subject. His findings are summarized in Table IV.

One significant finding in Table IV is that women expressed in all seven instances at least as much as, or more, intolerance than men. I then asked my own sample to *guess* public attitudes towards transsexualism. The significance of the differences

Sex Change

Table IV

PERCENTAGES OF MALES AND FEMALES INTOLERANT
OF TRANSSEXUALISM*

Aspects of Transsexualism	% of Males Intolerant	% of Females Intolerant
1. Should the conversion operation be available to transsexuals?	18% said no	18% said no
2. Would you feel at ease in the presence of a feminized trans-sexual?	38% said no	41% said no
3. Would you put a feminized trans-sexual with a woman roommate?	14% said no	22% said no
4. Should an operated transsexual be freely permitted to marry a man?	7% said no	7% said no
5. Should the operated transsexual be allowed to adopt a child?	21% said no	28% said no
6. Should the operated transsexual be permitted in occupations such as babysitting and teaching?	12% said no	16% said no
7. Is it better to permit the operation?	7% said no	8% said no

*Starke R. Hathaway, "Transsexual Questionnaire," (Unpublished) University of Minnesota.

between the guesses of males, females and transsexuals was tested by way of a Kruskal-Wallis analysis of variance, yielding a value of 7.19, which is significant beyond the .05 level. Women were found to *impute* the greatest intolerance to the public, and this makes sense, since Hathaway's data indicate women to *be* the most intolerant group in this regard. While men were found to impute less intolerance than women, it was the transsexual who imputed the least amount of intolerance. In other words, it is the transsexual who assumes that others are most accepting of her, while men and women are more correct in their appraisal of public attitudes in this regard.

We have seen that a number of significant differences exist between transsexuals, males and females. Transsexuals were found to be more feminine than the two other gender groups and also more conservative in their endorsement of traditional sex definitions. Consequently they are less aware of role strain in the area of sex roles than women. They also use sex and gender definitions which differ from those used by most of the male and female respondents, and it has been argued that this enables them to define themselves as real women. Finally, they impute less intolerance to the public than do men and women, and than is actually the case.

A Methodological Introduction to the Remainder of the Book

Thus far in the study we have used quantitative methods to compare transsexuals with males and females. However from here on our methodology, dictated by the aim of the study and the nature of the subject matter, will be different. At this point we must digress a bit in order to discuss the methodology of the next chapters.

The use of quantitative variable analysis has serious limitations, as Herbert Blumer already showed in 1956. The typical sociological study, Blumer pointed out, follows the classical research design and is deductive. That is, it starts from a given theoretical perspective, formulates certain hypotheses relating dependent and independent variables and proceeds to verify those hypotheses empirically by developing the proper methodology and operationalizations and by selecting the proper population and sample. The propositions that are supported by the facts are then conditionally accepted as valid explanations of a given behavior.

The limitations of this procedure are essentially two-fold. In the first place, sociological work based on variable analysis has not resulted in the integration of empirical findings and theory; it has not led to a body of formal theory consisting of propositions that have universal applicability. This is due to the disparate nature of our findings, the time- and place-boundness of our operationalizations, our lack of generic variables.

Secondly, it is questionable whether variable analysis is the appropriate model for the formulation of certain relevant questions and for the valid explanation of important aspects of group life. Although the validity of some explanations can be demonstrated adequately through variable analysis, the procedure does not enable us to deal with a highly relevant set of questions, namely an understanding of group life as it emerges through interpretative social processes. Thus, classical variable analysis, while answering the challenge of validity to some extent, does not provide theoretical integration and does not address itself to the problem of relevance.

There is a feeling that variable analysis has, in some ways, led to a dead-end; a feeling that we are not engaged in either meaningful research or theoretical growth. Nevertheless, most of us try to get out of the impasse by mere modifications in operationalizations, the refinement of measuring instruments and the retest of hypotheses under different conditions, among new populations. Blumer's critique of variable analysis implies that the way out of the impasse must be sought at a higher theoretical level. In this endeavor, sociologists must work from the center outward, so to speak. Since our most serious problem seems to be a widening irreconciliability between theory and research, the best thing to do at this point is to hold in abeyance both the formulation of a closed theoretical system and the use of one specific methodology. Such a procedure provides the best hope for the eventual integration of theory and research.

Only recently has progress along these lines been made. Ethnomethodology and symbolic interactionism can be seen as the methodological and the theoretical facets of the effort at breaking out of the impasse.* Although symbolic interactionism is fairly old by sociological standards, it remained academic until such men

---

*Norman Denzin (1969) compares symbolic interactionism and ethnomethodology, and suggests their possible synthesis. It is not clear whether Denzin views both symbolic interactionism and ethnomethodology as theories. Since it is also possible to view ethnomethodology as a form of ethnography, i.e. a technique rather than a theory, the statement made in the text may not be in conflict with Denzin's suggested synthesis of symbolic interactionism and ethnomethodology.

as Goffman and Garfinkel began to experiment along lines implied in Meadian theory.

Symbolic interactionism is generally called a theory, yet it is not a closed system, as for example Parsonian functionalism. While it is therefore more difficult to derive from that perspective hypotheses that may be tested through the use of variable analysis, the perspective at the same time offers the opportunity to ask some new questions. Symbolic interactionism's concern with the (inter-) subjective meaningful aspects of behavior is what makes it the most promising orientation.

Ethnomethodology is similarly characterized by a lack of firm conceptual commitment, in this case to a specific method of inquiry, and to the study of specific behaviors by specific groups. Central to Garfinkel's ethnomethodology (1967) seems to be the recommendation that any behavior is worth studying, including normal, routine, rational behavior, because all behavior consists of covert as well as overt meanings. Ethnomethodology's lack of commitment to preconceptions suggests greater leeway to the researcher when he encounters serendipitic findings and must revise his deductive propositions.

Ethnomethodology is an ambiguous word. It refers to an enterprise that is somewhat similar to a tradition quite old among anthropologists. Early ethnographers such as Malinowski already perceived the central task of their discipline to be *understanding of the native's point of view, his relation to life and his vision of the world.* This led to the subsequent development of ethnoscience, which tries to uncover a given society's folk classifications, its particular ways of classifying its material and social universe. This "new ethnography" is primarily emic, that is, it studies a given society's culture and classifications from within, not from the point of view of Western social science or any other perspective; it proceeds primarily through the componential analysis of language.

The convergences between the new ethnoscience in anthropology and ethnomethodology in sociology were discussed in an article by George Psathas (1969). Just as the ethnoscientist's emic analysis is an effort at getting "inside" events in order to see what kind of theory it is that the natives themselves use to organize phenomena in their daily lives, similarly the ethnomethodologist seeks to discover the "methods" that persons use in their everyday lives in society in constructing social reality, and also to discover the nature of the realities they have constructed.

It should be kept in mind that ethnomethodology does *not* refer to a new sociological method. While it does imply methods which will differ from classical variable analysis, the "-methodology" suffix in the term refers to the *methods which men use to make their world meaningful*. In Garfinkel's words, these are the methods used by men in society for producing and making accountable — to themselves and others — their everyday affairs. For example, Garfinkel describes the transsexual Agnes as a "practical methodologist," because her continuing studies of everyday activities are seen as "members' methods for producing correct decisions about normal sexuality in ordinary activities."

In addition, ethnomethodology is grounded in phenomenology, because it defines and approaches research problems in such a way as to result in the discovery of the essential features of the social phenomena being studied. By definition, the phenomenological position is one of "going to the things themselves," to the social phenomena rather than to previously developed theories to be tested by the formulation of deductive hypotheses. This position requires from the social scientist that he discover the under-standings that the actor and the other have of one another. This process has been called "intra-cultural verstehen," involving "socialization into the meanings of the members of the culture" (Wax, 1967). This is in clear convergence with symbolic inter-actionism's emphasis on empathy as a basic component of role-taking.

Both symbolic interactionism and ethnomethodology rely more on participant observation, possibly of the disguised type, than on survey research and structured questionnaires. Consequently, their findings may be more difficult to quantify and test statistically; findings may have to remain descriptive and documentary. Nevertheless, these approaches combine different methods and different methods of analysis. In addition, since the primary task here is *not* to understand behavior-in-the-laboratory, or behavior-in-the-sociologist's society, but behavior where it occurs in everyday life, there must be greater reliance on sensitizing concepts than on deductive hypotheses. Finally, since the ethnomethodologist wishes foremost to uncover the covert background relevancies that latently guide the members' behavior, he may have to experimentally induce disruptions and disturbances of role expectations. These, then, are some of the methodological implications of ethnomethodology.

What has been said about the limitations of variable analysis and the advantages of alternative approaches such as ethnomethodology applies a fortiori when dealing with an entirely new phenomenon embodied by a very limited number of people. Such is the case of the transsexual. In this case, no assumptions could be made about any population, the number of respondents was small, and the object of the study was obviously exploratory, not hypothesis testing. Quantitative tabulations and statistical tests of a priori hypotheses were contemplated but regarded potentially sterile. It was decided at this point that a study of a group of transsexuals can best proceed through the careful examination and presentation of the most significant data collected during the extended interviews, in the hope that some of the most salient aspects of the transsexual's postoperative life would emerge. The aspects that I had in mind during the empirical phase of the study are those that have been focused on by earlier students of sexual deviance, stigma management, status passage, identity conflict, and by ethnomethodologists who have been concerned with uncovering of the latent, tacit methods that people use in their everyday communications and interaction.

Social order, it is realized by a growing number of sociologists, is not to be assumed but to be explained. In fact, unlike the functionalists, whose tendency has been to assume and merely demonstrate the existence of the social order, sociology is now redefining its task in the only proper way possible. The question is not why there is deviance, misunderstanding, conflict and social breakdown, but precisely why concerted social action is possible.

Sociologists may have failed to realize the necessity to define their task in such a Hobbesian fashion because, up until recently, the social reality in which they operated consisted of well-integrated homogeneous social systems. However, due to changing societal and political conditions, conflict sociology is once again in the ascendancy and, along with it, a tendency no longer to take consensus and normative integration for granted, but to question them. The ethnomethodological study of routine as well as deviant behavior forms part of this tendency.

Transsexuals, like other deviants, provide another area in which the central sociological question can be posed: How is meaningful, consensual interaction possible between different groups and different individuals, in this case individuals whose sexual experience sets them far apart from most others in terms of their role expectations and role behavior, cultural definitions and self-definitions, learning experience and accomplishments, motivations and goals? In brief, what is the nature of the transsexual's relationship to society?

It has been shown that transsexuals share certain features with one another which contrast them with nontranssexuals. This, however, is merely a starting point. What remains to be done is to show that some transsexuals are knocking on the doors of the dominant middle-class society while others among them remain more separatist; that some are more marginal to middle-class society than others; that, over and beyond their ambitions, some are more successful at gaining access to the dominant society than others; that each transsexual uses whatever methods and means she has in order to obtain rewards from society; that these rewards can take the form of financial success, social acceptance, psychological security, or a combination of these and other factors.

The next four chapters will enable us to look at composite portraits of different types of transsexuals.

REFERENCES

Benjamin, Harry: Nature and management of transsexualism, with a report on 31 operated cases. Western Journal of Surgery, Obstetrics and Gynecology, 72:105-111, 1964.
––– The Transsexual Phenomenon. New York, Julian Press, 1966.
Blumer, Herbert: Sociological analysis and the variable. Am Sociol Rev, December: 683-690, 1956.
Denzin, Norman K.: Symbolic interactionism and ethnomethodology: A

proposed synthesis. Am Sociol Rev, December: 922-934, 1969.

Driscoll, James P.: Transsexuals. Transaction (March-April). Special Supplement. pp. 28-37, 66, 68, 1971.

Garfinkel, Harold: Studies in Ethnomethodology. Englewood Cliffs, N.J., Prentice Hall, 1967, pp. 116-185.

Goffman, Erving: Stigma: Notes on the Management of Spoiled Identity. Englewood Cliffs, N.J., Prentice Hall, 1963.

Goode, William J.: A theory of role strain. Am J Sociol, August, 1960.

Hamburger, Christian; Sturup, George K., and Dahl-Iversen, E.: Transvestism: Hormonal, psychiatric and surgical treatment. JAMA, 152:391-396, 1953.

Hathaway, Starke R.: Transsexual questionnaire. (Unpublished), 1968.

Jorgensen, Christine: A Personal Autobiography. New York, Bantam Books, 1968.

Money, John: Cytogenics of transvestism and transsexualism. Journal of Sex Research, May: 141-144, 1967.

Psathas, George: Ethnomethodology and phenomenology. Social Research, April:500-520, 1969.

Siegel, Sidney: Nonparametric Statistics for the Behavioral Sciences. New York, McGraw-Hill, 1956, pp. 184-193.

Stoller, Robert J.: Sex and Gender: On the Development of Masculinity and Femininity. New York, Science House, 1968.

Stone, Gregory P.: Appearance and the Self. In Rose, Arnold (Ed.): Human Behavior and Social Processes. Boston, Houghton Mifflin, 1962, pp. 86-118.

Walinder, J.: Transsexualism: A Study of Forty-three Cases. Goteborg, Scandinavian University Books, 1967.

Wax, M. L.: On misunderstanding Verstehen: A reply to Abel. Sociology and Social Research, 51:323-333, 1967.

Worden, Frederick G., and Marsh, James T.: Psychological factors in men seeking sex transformation. JAMA, 157:1292-1298, 1955.

Chapter 3

(A TYPOLOGY
OF TRANSSEXUALS)

 A FTER their release from the hospital, the feminized transsexuals work at various forms of postoperative adjustment. That is, they begin to develop and then routinize a certain relationship with the dominant society. While it is too early to tell whether any transsexual's present lifestyle is permanent,* distinctions can nevertheless already be made. It was possible, at the time of the interviews, to discern at least the following four types of postoperative adjustment: the housewife type, the showbusiness type, the aspiring housewife, and the career woman. These are, of course, constructs to which transsexuals never totally conform. Nevertheless, in spite of overlap, the four types do represent distinct alternative lifestyles followed by different transsexuals. What follows is a discussion of the types and composite portraits based on the answers of transsexuals most typical of each type.

Sally: The Housewife

Some transsexuals, as we saw, have been able to pass as natural-born females more easily than others because their surgical feminization was more successful. In general, these transsexuals were fairly young at the time of their conversion operation and

---

*The University of Minnesota team that initiated the transsexual project — led by Drs. Donald Hastings and Starke R. Hathaway of the Department of Psychiatry — is currently engaged in a ten-year follow-up study of these patients. Their findings will be published at the end of this period.

they had engaged in a considerable amount of anticipatory socialization in female sex roles through cross-dressing. In addition, they had generally been operated upon earlier than the other transsexuals, so that they had more time to adjust to their new lives as females.

By the time our interviews started, many of these transsexuals had definitely opted for a middle-class way of life. This meant that most of them wished to dissociate themselves from other transsexuals as well as from transvestites, homosexuals, and the entire underworld urban subculture centering around striptease, prostitution, homosexuality, and other forms of deviant or commercialized sexuality. These transsexuals' ultimate goal was to become married, adopt children and settle down, preferably in suburbia, for a life-long role of "average housewife." Ideally, this group would end up passing altogether, so that eventually nobody or only a very few intimate friends and relatives would know of their sex change.

At the time of the interviews, four transsexuals were already married, thus indicating at least partial success toward the fulfillment of this ideal. It should be pointed out, however, that three of them were married to exconvicts, suggesting that the pool of available mates remained restricted to a marginal and deviant population, preventing transsexuals from transscending their original milieu and from definitively moving out into middle-class respectability.

Nevertheless, this group's goals were clear, and partial fulfillment of these goals was a distinct possibility. It is also this group that may have contributed most heavily to the transsexuals' overall conservatism in the area of sex roles and sex norms, since they conceived of the role of housewife, domesticity and supportive functions as the ultimate fulfillment of a woman, while relegating roles of leadership and economic responsibility to the male partner. These young and attractive transsexuals, these housewife types, valued domesticity, middle-class respectability and heterosexual monogamy.

Sally epitomized this orientation. She had been feminized quite early in the project, nearly two years ago. When she arrived at my office for our first interview, she was well-dressed, but the relative simplicity of her attire and make-up was a contrast to the appearance of many transsexuals interviewed subsequently. Sally was twenty-seven, tall and blonde. Her complexion was smooth, her voice feminine, her face not unattractive. Her miniskirt revealed fairly feminine legs. Having cross-dressed before her operation for a number of years, she had had ample time and experience to develop feminine mannerisms. She seemed quite happy, somewhat over-active, talking to various members of the hospital staff. She apologized for being late, and we began to discuss her background:

"Well," she began, "I was born and raised in a small town in Minnesota. My parents are Lutheran, but that doesn't affect me. . . . I never saw much of my father, he worked nights and slept days; I was mother's pet, I guess. My mother is a very domineering person; she wore the pants in the family. . . . I have two brothers and a sister, now it's two sisters and a brother." [She laughs. One of the people Sally is referring to is her sister Elizabeth, another transsexual in our sample. Sally and Elizabeth claim to be the only siblings in the world to have both undergone sex change.]

"When did you move to the Twin Cities?" I asked.

"I moved to Saint Paul when I finished high school. Elizabeth, my sister, was already living there so I moved in with her, until the operation. . . ."

"How did your family react to the fact that both you and Elizabeth underwent sex surgery?"

"My mother is the one who took the operations the hardest. She had always been proud of giving birth to a first-born son. After the operation my parents disowned me, Elizabeth too; they don't want us to visit home. That's off-limits. . . ."

"How do you feel about that?"

"Well, they are just ignorant people; they can't understand how I feel, how grateful I am to the doctors. . . . I'm still in touch with my brother, but my parents are just simple people. . . ."

"Who underwent sex change first, you or Elizabeth?"

"She did."

"Did you decide to do it together?"

"Well, not exactly . . . but we have always been very close; we both wanted it, all along. . . ."

Sally then began to discuss her recent life, the fact that she met John shortly after her release from the hospital, and what happened then.

"I met him right after the operation, at a party, and we got married right away. So that's when I moved out of Elizabeth's house. . . . John spent three years in prison for arson, but he is real good now. He is a real hard worker; he is going back to night school, too! I love him very much. He is so gentle and so good to me . . . he is the most important thing that ever happened to me."

"How does he feel about your sex change?"

"He doesn't know. . . ."

Startled by this revelation, I asked how this was possible and whether it might lead to difficulties in the future. Sally's answer was evasive but definite on one point: "I never want him to find out! He might have the marriage annulled!"

The interview then moved on to Sally's attitudes toward men and women in general.

"Women," she said, "are more fearful of us than men. They fear that we'll be able to please a man better than they would, since we were men ourselves. . . ."

"Does that mean that you still think of yourself as a man, at times?"

"Never. Even before the operation I was always identified as a woman. I went dressed as a woman, used women's bathrooms."

"What do you consider the ultimate criterion of being a woman?"

"It's feeling and acting like a woman. A woman should be a good wife, being able to make a man happy, sexually and otherwise; I agree that her place is in the kitchen. . . ."

"How about having children?"

"Well, that's not what makes a woman . . . I want to adopt children, of course. . . . Maybe someday they'll have an operation for that, too. . . . Anyway it's possible to be physically a man and yet truly a woman. It's one's personality, mind, outlook, that make the difference. . . ."

I then asked Sally some questions about her relationship to other transsexuals. Here is what she had to say about that: "Well of course I know most of them. You know, 'birds of a feather flock together.' I met most of them here at the hospital (I had to come back for corrective surgery a couple of times). But socially I don't see them hardly at all. I only see Elizabeth. When the two of us are together we are sensible, but when more of us are around, well you see, we don't always get along, we hinder each other, we don't behave well en masse. Once in a while we chat, our conversations are technical, mostly about the surgery. But I've talked about this surgery enough. I don't want to talk about it all my life. . . .

"Many of them live very unmoralistic lives; they go through a sexual binge after their operation. This is their way to find out how much a woman they are. I guess we are all exhibitionists after our operation, and this builds self-confidence; but most trans-sexuals here in Minneapolis have no moral standards. Some of them are strippers downtown and they advertise themselves. They are sex changes; I'm merely a correction. The words 'sex change' and 'transsexual' are very offensive to me. I can't identify with these terms. Most other transsexuals move around quite a bit, two are in Hawaii, two are in Canada; quite a few are on welfare. I think most of them are pigs. Most transsexuals only love themselves. So I can see why men categorize all of us as pigs. My sister and I are different. You see, I feel that I am better than the other ones, I have better morals. . . . There are many transsexuals who I feel much more uneasy with than with straights . . . all my friends are straight."

Sally apparently wanted to dissociate herself from other transsexuals and from the underworld subculture with which most transsexuals have been affiliated. She accused other transsexuals of loose living and loose morality, while taking exception to this for herself. The utilization of fellow transsexuals as a negative reference group highlights an important facet of the transsexual conversion: as true converts, the housewife types reacted emotionally and negatively to their past experiences, identities and social milieus. Psychologically, their passage into middle-class respectability required this.

Thus, while a majority of transsexuals had been transvestites and homosexuals before their operations, the housewife types and, in fact, most other transsexuals as well, now frowned severely upon these forms of behavior, refusing even to define their former homosexual and transvestite acts as such. Here is what Sally had to say about that:

"I hate homos! I never wanted sex with them. I had homosexual affairs in grade school and in high school, but only with normals. I was never a homosexual in any form. I never went to gay bars; I was not accepted by gay society, nor did I wish to be. My affairs with men were one-sided; I played a passive role. I derived no pleasure from them, because I felt I was a woman. When I cross-dressed it didn't do anything to me sexually, either. I wasn't a transvestite, you see. . . . On stage I was effeminate, but otherwise, no. I think homos are pigs. I no longer tolerate them. I don't even want to read about them. Homos get what they deserve! All my friends are heteros. . . ."

Sally's general conservatism became more pronounced yet when she took the masculinity-femininity test. It revealed her strong endorsement of traditional sex definitions and the double standard of sexual morality ("premarital sex relations are more permissible for men than for women"). She strongly supported traditional stereotypes of masculinity and femininity ("Men must be bold while women should conform;" "women must be gentle, men must be strong;" "women have a greater desire to have children than do men;" "men should do most of the talking, women should listen;" "men are generally happy to be men, but quite a few women would actually prefer to be men;" "men are rational, women are emotional;" "men must be brave, competitive, active, knowledgeable, *etc.*" while "women must be shy, cooperative, submissive, physically attractive and young.")

Sally was also in overwhelming agreement with the current division of labor in society, prescribing such occupations as medicine, law, science, the military and law enforcement to men, and such occupations as teaching, nursing, social work, cafe waiting and other helping professions to women. At one point she said, "A woman has no business making money driving a cab, or anything like that, unless there is something wrong with her!" She added, "I don't think men and women should make the same amount of money. A man should make more than a woman! Business executives should be strictly men . . . men should be the leaders!"

Sally described herself, on another part of the scale, as "emotional, conforming, adaptable and extremely gentle." She subscribed to various fashion magazines and confession magazines, while being ignorant of such male publications as *Playboy* and *Esquire*. She said that she was not interested in cars, sports and politics, but that cooking had always been one of her interests.

The clearest expression of Sally's overall orientation, however, occurred on one occasion when I picked her up at home for an afternoon of informal conversation and meetings with some colleagues. The setting was typical. She had been preparing a meal for her husband who was at work. I waited in the living room while she was getting ready, which would "only take a minute" but became nearly an hour. Getting dressed and made up, to Sally and to most other transsexuals, was more important, elaborate and time-consuming than to most women. Yet, when I complimented her on the beautiful simplicity of her make-up, she said, "John doesn't want me to look like a slut, like these other transsexuals, so I don't use much make-up or anything fancy." (Luckily, she had very little facial hair).

These last comments get at Sally's basic self-concept, her total embracement of the role of submissive housewife. Before leaving her apartment, various household chores had to be completed or else, she said, John would be displeased when returning from work:

"You know how men are," she said, ". . . but I love him, he is really considerate; he works for [a local manufacturer], so I don't have to work anymore. I'm a housewife now! He has gained forty pounds since we got married, so he must like my cooking! I always do as he says; I think all women should ultimately submit to their husband's decisions. I submit to John and I have always submitted to males. . . ."

In line with her drive to establish middle-class domesticity and respectability, Sally placed a high premium on privacy. At this time, very few people know of her sex change. She had successfully protected her privacy. Only her family and the doctors knew. I asked her whether she ever disclosed her sex change to anyone voluntarily. Her reply: "Well, sometimes I have to, like when I applied for a new name at City Hall. But otherwise no . . . I would never tell my children for instance."

Sally, then, typifies the housewife type, both in terms of her actual accomplishments to date, and in her values and attitudes. Her husband may be a former inmate, and her lifestyle may not be entirely middle-class (they live in a fairly dilapidated part of the city, not far from skidrow), but overall she is clearly trying to establish, and is, in fact, establishing for herself and her husband a life of domesticity, regularity and respectability.

As suggested earlier, no transsexual is either entirely within or totally outside the housewife pattern. The differences are gradual. The extent to which they share ambitions of domestic fulfillment varies from realistic objectives already partly achieved to remote future dreams that may never be realized. In any event, all transsexuals experience situations in which they try to de-emphasize their sex change and attempt to pass as natural-born females in order to gain the social acceptance which eludes them as long as their stigma is known. The main difference is that some of them have moved considerably further in this direction than others, and some may, perhaps realistically, never actively pursue this course to its full extent.

Thus, another attractive young transsexual, Maryjo, while now employed as a stripper in a Minneapolis nightclub (hardly a symptom of middle-class adjustment), nevertheless also shares elements of this syndrome. She maintains that this is only temporary and that she wishes to leave town and start a new life of respectability as soon as possible: "I hope to get out soon . . . like I don't want to advertise myself; I run into too many people [who know]. I'm only waiting for my birth certificate to be changed."

Maryjo's greatest wish is to adopt children, and when asked whether she had ever been married, she replied: "Only engaged, twice . . . but a wedding ring is what counts!"

A final note of interest about this group of transsexuals is that several of them marry, postoperatively, their former homosexual partners. Pat, for example, a quiet and somewhat stocky blonde in her mid-twenties, became married shortly after her sex change to the man she had been living with in homosexual union for four years. This pattern — two homosexuals transforming their relationship into a heterosexual one through the conversion operation of one partner — represents a tendency to normalize and legitimize the relationship. Patricia, like many other transsexuals, maintains that her sexual relationships have never been homosexual ones, since she was in effect always a woman, the surgery merely setting straight a minor aberration of nature. Her husband, she says, has always been very influential on her. "We agreed that I should get the operation . . . he urged me . . . it's much better now."

Renee and Lisa: The Strippers

A number of transsexuals, far from aiming at middle-class respectability and homely domesticity, have opted for a career in underworld showbusiness, appearing in various nightclubs as strippers and dancers, sometimes advertising themselves as sex changes, sometimes engaging in prostitution on the side. While many transsexuals currently thus employed also pay lip service to middle-class standards of sex behavior and stereotypes of proper masculinity and femininity, ultimately hoping to join the housewives in their mode of adjustment, some have few qualms about exploiting their newly acquired femininity for immediate financial gain. What is more, some realize, perhaps realistically, that this is the best bargain they can ever hope for. There is, then, a group of transsexuals for whom status passage into the dominant society and its lifestyles is a less urgent objective.

Christine Jorgensen is on many transsexuals' minds. The first man ever to receive a conversion operation in the history of modern medicine became, as a result, wealthy, famous and allegedly happy. Christine's autobiography depicts her conversion as a transition from a miserable suicidal misfit into a rich, happy jetsetter. Other early sex changes reaped similar benefits from media exposure. Shalimar, for example, became a well-known and wealthy nightclub dancer appearing in various parts of the world.

Jorgensen, then, and other early sex changes who became celebrities in showbusiness, embody a role model that has influenced many transsexuals in their decisions. This emerged clearly from the interviews.

In the first place, some former female impersonators may have consciously requested the conversion operation in order to become a greater attraction in showbusiness. Secondly, whether this was a motive for undergoing the operation or not, several ended up appearing on stage as sex changes. Thirdly, the showbusiness type also includes transsexuals appearing in night-clubs as bona fide females. These individuals may not advertise themselves to the public as sex changes, but their occupation as nightclub strippers or dancers also constitutes a commercialization of their newly acquired womanhood. Finally, some feminized transsexuals operate as prostitutes, and while this, too, is generally passing behavior (the client is generally unaware of the prostitute's sex change), it also represents the financial exploitation of the new gender identity.

In sum there is a group of transsexuals who do not behave according to middle-class standards of morality, because they opt for the immediate monetary rewards to be gained from their newly acquired femininity, rather than the respectability and social acceptance that are sought after by the housewife type. This group often operates in the shady regions of showbusiness, some being prostitutes on the side, and they envy and wish to emulate the career of such successful transsexuals as Christine Jorgensen. Hence, this type may be called the showbusiness type or Jorgensen type.

While there may be a correlation between passing and the two types — the housewife tending to pass more as a natural-born female than the showbusiness type — this correlation is imperfect at best. More often than not, prostitutes and strippers pass as natural-born females on the job. The difference, of course, is that the housewife wishes to pass into roles and statuses of middle-class femininity, while the stripper and the prostitute merely pass from the extreme category of transsexualism into less severely deviant roles associated with the underworld. It should also be noted that many showbusiness types are among the young, attractive and highly successfully feminized transsexuals. Understandably, those physical prerequisites are as important for this type of adjustment as for the housewife type. In sum, the showbusiness type, or the stripper type, is the transsexual who sees advantages in her predicament, making as it were a virtue of a vice.

A prime example of this mode of adjustment was Renee. She was an extremely beautiful young woman about whose femininity there could be no doubt. Her body seemed god-given rather than man-made. She was dark-skinned, dark-haired and twenty-eight at the time of our first meeting. This took place during break at her nightclub. Renee's slender and well-shaped body was considerably exposed at this time, and her voice and mannerisms were totally feminine. She first misunderstood my approach, taking me for a potential client. A brief exchange revealed that she was extremely wealthy, living in a plush suite in one of the city's most expensive hotels, practicing prostitution to supplement her income. Once I explained to her what my aim was, she seemed to cool off, perhaps bored, perhaps suspicious of the sociologist, in any event silent not from shyness, but from a tough underworld attitude dictating suspicion toward established investigators. Better rapport was established later, after her act.

I learned that Renee was born and raised in rural Minnesota, in a lower-class family. Her father was an unskilled worker, the family was Lutheran ("but I'm a free believer now!" she emphasized). This information was given in speech and mannerisms that were clearly lower-class. Fancy words like "rational" and "disclosure" had to be explained to her. Somewhat surprisingly, Renee did complete high school. She then went to a beauty college, graduating in 1963. She proudly told how, when she was seventeen and eighteen, in high school, she had been champion baton twirler, winning "eighty-three trophies and forty-two medals" and teaching her skill to "hundreds of students." She had her first homosexual experiences in high school and began cross-dressing at nineteen, as she was entering beauty college. She has lived as a woman ever since, performing as a female impersonator in night clubs around the nation and abroad. She is now a Catholic, but only since 1966, when she converted to that faith for her boyfriend's sake. She works as a dancer and stripper in a downtown nightclub, advertising herself as a sex change. In addition to striptease, her act involves the use of fire batons and Samoan knives, thus using the skills learned as a high school baton twirler.

Renee was one of the first transsexuals to undergo surgery, and the operation was immediately successful. Unlike most other patients, she did not have to return to the hospital for corrections, only for vaginal dilation. She attributes the outstanding quality of her sex surgery to the fact that she was operated on by a different surgeon than most other transsexuals, a surgeon with exceptional competence. Our interview first dealt with that aspect. Having thanked her for her cooperation and having received the icy reply that her "life was an open book, anyway," I proceeded to compliment her about her looks and steered the conversation toward the surgical aspects of her sex change.

"Thank you," she said. "I know I look young. I have a young body, and the doctors have said so! I was one of the first ones, two years ago. I had a different surgeon. He is in Vietnam now. He was much better than the other ones, as a surgeon, and also cosmetically! It took him nine hours, and they sent me home after nine days. . . ."

"What prompted you to request the operation in the first place?" I asked.

"Well, I just had to find out that I could be helped. Working in showbusiness I had the knowledge that I could go to Casablanca, but I couldn't afford it, and I was afraid because it was out of this country; that would be a long trip and a lot of money. . . ."

"But what was your primary reason for undergoing the sex change? Sexual, psychological, social?"

"It was mostly a matter of social acceptance. I was rejected by both heteros and homos; I didn't fit anywhere."

"How did your family react?"

"I have no trouble from them . . . probably because of the type of life I lead, because I am in showbusiness and the type of people I frequent. I don't mix my family with them, or with my friends . . . although I've brought some of my acquaintances home with me. . . . I've lived with my family all my life. But you'll be surprised. All my life, like in high school, I felt like an outcast, people were on my back, I felt different. You got a mark put on you for being feminine . . . I was very effeminate. . . . I have seven brothers and sisters. They have had quite a bit to say about my operation . . . they are the ones who decided on my new names. . . . When my sister got married there were four hundred guests and six bridesmaids; I was one of them!"

"So, you get along fine with your family?"

"Yes. My family respects my judgment and trusts me."

"How about your boyfriend?" (Renee had mentioned that she was not married by dated steadily).

"Well, we have been dating for three years. I became Catholic because he was Catholic, and now I am his girlfriend. . . ."

"Did he urge you to undergo the sex surgery?"

"Well, we sort of agreed that I should . . . I am independent. I have been engaged twice since my surgery."

Renee's sex life was complex. On the one hand she was one of the transsexuals who underwent sex change in order to normalize, heterosexualize and make socially more acceptable an otherwise durable homosexual relationship. On the other hand, it turned out, her sex life was not now monogamous, nor had it been before the operation.

"How was dating before the operation?" I asked.

"I dated girls for the front, that's all. I never had sex with them."

"Did you date men?"

"Oh yes, but not openly."

"When did you begin cross-dressing?"

"Well, I have been a female impersonator since 1963 . . . I did it all over, in Washington, New York, Japan, Denver. . . . I was a female impersonator because this was the closest way I could be what I wanted to be in the eyes of the law, legally. I lived as a female for seven years. I even had two successful businesses that I owned and operated as a woman. Even some of my lovers didn't ever find out. I was never a homosexual. I went to gay bars twice in my entire life. I was never a part of gay society. . . ."

"Now you are legally a woman, aren't you?"

"Not yet, but I have an appointment with my lawyer tomorrow. He has had the papers since before the operation. I could have changed my name a year ago, but I was out of work and on welfare and I got this bad situation. . . . My first name now was my stage name before. I also changed my last name, because it was my former stage name, it was too well-known. My middle name is my sister's first name."

"How about your former names?"

"I can't stand those names, but it's not my fault. I wasn't the one who named me. I wish I'd never had them! My middle name was. . . . Doesn't that sound terrible? I am very sensitive on that subject because I want to forget those names!"

Do you have any plans for moving?"

"I hope to get out soon . . . I have been living here for a long time, unfortunately. . . . I don't want to advertise myself, I run into too many people I know. Eventually maybe if they don't know me right away, maybe my sex change wouldn't be known. . . .I hope to get out, but first I have to make the money for a new start. . . ."

"How many people know?"

"Well, it's like this: for the first three months no one knew. Then, gradually, one person told another. As you know I am in showbusiness. Now at work everyone knows, of course. I know it sounds funny, I should be around more people who don't know, but it's a fear right now, maybe because it's still too new to be around people who don't know. . . . Off the job I only disclose it if someone really puts it on me, like if they find out from someone else and keep questioning me, then there is no point in me pretending and trying to lie."

"Who would you be most reluctant to disclose it to?"

"To strangers. If I ever got married my husband would have to know or else I couldn't live with him. It would only be fair to him and if he loved me enough it would be alright. I don't want to disclose it to anybody of course, but sometimes you have to . . . they'd have to be someone I could trust. . . . My children will know that I had corrective surgery but I wouldn't mention exactly what it was."

Apparently Renee was not very much involved in the process of passing. While she shared with other transsexuals ambitions of marriage, motherhood and status passage, her current situation was one in which she was mostly known to be a sex change, and she did not (yet) actively seek to pass as a respectable and natural-born female. Her "up front" attitude towards her true identity was further evidenced when I asked her how she related to other transsexuals, to which she replied:

"I don't socialize too much with other transsexuals. They tend to be cliquish. All we do when we see each other is discuss the surgery — 'this doctor did this to me, and that doctor did that to me, I have to go back for a check-up.' It gets to the point where you don't want to hear all that all the time. . . . In general I would rather talk of a corrective operation. . . . Other transsexuals would understand what I am talking about, but if I talked to someone else who knows, like my roommate, I would have to explain. . . .

"Right now I am living in an apartment building with nothing but girls. It's all girl talk, but there is a problem, you know how society looks down on strippers, and we are all dancers at the house. . . . Anyway, I am a little sensitive about this because of the way society has made jokes of it, and I've been made a joke of most of my life, and I'm getting tired of it. Because people — they don't really know. But as long as they don't interfere with my personal life I couldn't care less. . . . We have individual personalities too, you know! We don't all think completely the same. We want to be seen as individuals, as women in the world!"

"How about acceptance, in general?"

"I find that if a person doesn't know, I'm accepted beautifully, but if someone tells them, there is this little thing in their mind . . . especially with other women. If they know, they want to feel superior to me. A woman in her mind feels superior because she was born this way and she can have children, and that's such a sad thing . . . I would love to have children."

"Who are more accepting in general, men or women?"

"Most men are very narrow-minded. Women are definitely more tolerant, because they are more emotional and they are a little bit more liberal."

"Who would feel more at ease with you, a man or a woman?"

"Most people would have to get used to you. . . . Anything that anybody doesn't understand, they want to destroy. If they don't know, there is no ill feeling at all. . . . But I don't know what goes on in men's minds! I think women are more tolerant."

"Who would be more opposed to your adopting a child, men or women?"

"Here goes the superiority feeling of women. In this case women would be less tolerant. Yet I feel that people who have had corrective surgery would make good mothers — most of them. I feel that if I get married they would have to accept the adoption of children. . . . The women that I know and that have met transsexuals think of us as good mothers. . . ."

Apparently Renee felt some societal rejection as a transsexual, and more so from men than women.* I then asked her whether anyone ever mistook her for a member of the opposite sex.

She answered: "A man? Never! . . . oh wait. On the phone sometimes, when my voice is low, they say 'yes sir,' but that even happens to my cousin."

"Do *you* ever think of yourself as a member of the opposite sex?"

"I want to honestly think about that. . . . Only with people who still think of me as a man. People that know and sit there and keep reminding me of what I am, and then I try to find out if they are right or not . . . but this is a hard question to answer."

"What do you consider the ultimate difference between a man and a woman?"

"Having sex organs . . . a vagina. I wish it was possible to have children, because that would be the difference . . . anyway the physical is very important. There are lots of masculine women, but this doesn't make them males. Being able to bear children is not what makes the difference either . . . look at all the women with hysterectomy! I can love my children as much as if I had gone through childbirth. . . ."

"You consider yourself a woman?"

"I *have* to . . . I do, because before I had surgery I was already what I am now. . . . But not being able to bear children kind of throws a lock on it because I wish I could, very much."

---

*For data on public response to transsexualism, and on the differential attitudes of men, women, and transsexuals toward this entire issue, see Kando, T.: The projection of intolerance: A comparison of males, females and transsexuals. *Journal of Sex Research,* August, 1972

In spite of the motherliness in Renee, she was by and large more the "liberated" type than the traditional female type. The masculinity-femininity scale revealed attitudes markedly different from those of a housewife type such as Sally. For example, Renee disagreed sharply with a great many stereotypical sex ascriptions. Neither did she agree that such occupations as social work, pediatrics, secretary and waitressing are most appropriate for women, and that such literature as *Playboy* and *Esquire* magazines are most appropriate for men. In fact, she commented that "women get as many kicks out of dirty magazines as men!" Her self-analysis, finally, was ambiguous, attributing to herself both male and female characteristics. For example, she admitted to being tough, but added this comment: "I have had to have my defenses up all my life. I want that explained. I don't agree that I'm tough, but society calls that tough, in fact I was always a rebel and that's why."

She also claimed to be competitive, self-controlled, talkative, and career oriented. In her own words: "I like domestic security, but right now, my work is more important to me than my home, because I am in showbusiness. I sleep days, work at night, dancing till one o'clock in the morning. I don't even talk to people, only when I am out in the audience, sitting with customers."

Renee, finally, was a very sexual person, acting and feeling young, and above all wanting to enjoy her youthful good looks more than to settle down. As she phrased it: ". . . I feel I have been cheated of so much in life, and now I don't feel my age. . . . I feel I'm only one year old, I feel I was reborn. I am young yet and I am going to enjoy life for a while."

Such casualness and lack of concern about respectability were typical of the strippers, not the housewives. By middle-class standards, Renee's morality could be termed loose. She had remote ambitions of settling down, but thus far, two years after her surgery, she was still a stripper. What is more, she *chose* the showbusiness route. As an extremely beautiful girl of twenty-eight, she was in no hurry to settle down. The sex change simply enabled her to enjoy life, youth, glamour, money and success, with no strings attached. Of all the transsexuals I met, Renee was no doubt the richest and the most glamorous. She embodied the most positive possibilities of her type of postoperative adjustment, and the fact that she was mentioned by a number of other respondents with envy indicates that she like Christine Jorgensen, may have functioned as a role model to those undergoing the conversion operation subsequently.

That some transsexuals are not as eagerly working toward middle-class adjustment is the result not only of an awareness of more immediate rewards to be gained from the commercial exploitation of the sex change itself, but also of a realistic appraisal of their chances at making it. Lisa, for example, was a huge fifty-five-year-old baritone-voiced nightclub performer, well aware of her limitations as a woman and of the unlikelihood of ever passing. Her situation was not as rosy as Renee's. Lisa, too, advertised herself openly as a sex change, but she was considerably older and less attractive. In fact, there was something grim about this fifty-five-year-old masculine woman. Her nightclub was a second-rate cafe featuring prostitution as well, and she was a freakish curiosity rather than an attraction. During our interviews, she turned out to be a sensitive, warm and intelligent woman.

Our first meeting took place in my hospital office. Lisa's size alone made it difficult to maintain equanimity when first meeting her. I estimate her height at six feet two inches and her weight at two hundred and twenty pounds. At this time, she was wearing a miniskirt revealing muscular legs and blonde hair done up in an elaborate chignon above her head, further enhancing her size. Her voice was very low. Very heavy make-up had not succeeded in hiding a rough complexion.

Her arrival for the first interview was characterized by all the pomp of an extrovert who has operated in showbusiness much of her life and who demands the full attention of whatever entourage she finds herself in. On this occasion, she was accompanied by a self-effacing young man about half her size, her current boyfriend as it turned out. Lisa dealt with the doctors and the hospital staff as she would with her nightclub audience, calling most of us "honey" and laughing and chatting loudly with whoever happened to be present.

We finally got down to business and she told me that she was born in Chicago, from Jewish parents, that she never finished high school and that her father, a small-store owner, died when she was fourteen. Also, she had been married three times but none of her marriages were consummated. Most of her life had centered around nightclubs. She had been a female impersonator for many years before her operation. As with the other transsexuals, part of the interview dealt with marriage. I asked Lisa to tell me something about her former marriages, her present marital status and her future plans. Here is some of what she said:

"Honey, I'm engaged to three guys. I prefer it that way. I was married to a woman before the operation, but marriage was never consummated. I was married three times, at sixteen, at eighteen and at thirty-eight. I never consummated any of them. I wanted to be something else. My wives were rich, they supported me. Then they got tired of waiting and got divorces. There were no hard feelings on either side. I don't know what they are doing now. They took care of the divorces. My first marriage lasted only a month, the second only three months, the third one a year."

"What about now? What are your plans?"

". . . I am going with this boy. He is twenty-two. He wants to marry me. . . ."

I asked Lisa whether she was going to accept the proposition. She was evasive, just as she was when I urged her to express her attitudes towards marriage in general. She did not seem to be too worried about her present lifestyle. In fact, she seemed quite happy. However, she had serious physiological and sexual problems, and she realized her inadequacies in that department.

"On the telephone they mistake me for a man several times a day. . . . That doesn't bother me too much, but my operation is not successful. . . . I had surgery on September 30, 1968. I stayed at the hospital for two months; I was very sick, I had complications, urine problems. They don't want me to come back for corrective surgery because I am too old. Now I have everything but it doesn't work. I have lost my sex desire anyway, I'm too afraid."

"Do you have any regrets?"

"No! I am very happy being a woman . . . I wish I could use my box though. I am not as young as the rest of them. I got to do it now!"

"What was the primary reason that you requested the operation?"

"It was primarily psychological. I found that I was a beautiful woman trapped in a fat man's body."

"Who did you discuss this with, before you decided to go through with the operation?"

"My boyfriend, a couple of close friends, but most of all my sister. My sister said to me, 'Very few people get a second chance. Go ahead and do it!' "

I asked Lisa about her current social life.

She replied, "I have about twenty real good friends. They are scattered all over the United States . . . I have family in Los Angeles. . . . After my surgery I moved out of Minneapolis. Here everybody knew me. Now I work up in. . . . I love it. I love all the Ukranians; the American male is so ignorant. I first went to Canada for two weeks and I have been staying there for three months. That's different. The U.S. is such a stiff country. In Canada they don't even look at me. Here everybody stares. But I don't care, people are paying to see me, I am not paying to see them."

"How are your relations with other transsexuals?"

"Well, when we are together, we sort of let our hair down, you know. You don't have to be on your guard . . . we sometimes horse around. If someone cuts me down I just say, 'You're just jealous because they cut more of me than of you.' But I only joke with gay boys. I wouldn't talk that way to strangers. . . ."

Lisa seemed fairly well entrenched in the marginal subculture of transsexuals, gay bars and stripjoints, even though she, too, derived immense pleasure from "going straight" and passing as a woman, as we saw from her description of her current life.

She went on to say, "I was a female impersonator for eighteen years, one of the most famous ones in America. Now, at the airport, people ask me, 'Aren't you. . . .?' So I say no and I show all my papers!" (She proudly showed her passport and driver's license, pointing out that they are legally feminized).

Lisa's urge to go straight also manifested itself when she criticized other transsexuals: "I think it's disgusting to advertise yourself as a sex change, like Renee. She is a fool to advertise herself like that . . . at her age she shouldn't be doing that! With me, I spend most of my spare time preparing my act, my jokes, but they don't know. . . . Some of the other transsexuals have no morals. . . . I have never been promiscuous; before the operation I always went steady with one guy at a time."

And when asked what she felt to be the essence of womanhood, Lisa gave further indication of her wish for moderation and respectability: "The most important thing is to behave like a woman . . . no, behave like a *lady*, not a woman. I am very class conscious. I want all the respect that's due a woman."

Thus, Lisa at fifty-five seemed ambivalent about the advantages of going the showbusiness route. Her criticism of Renee implied that if she had to do it again, twenty years younger, she might go the housewife route. Nevertheless, the overall picture remained that of a raw, lower-class individual, well aware of her limitations as a respectable lady but happy to take advantage of her sex change in other ways. For one thing, even though during one part of the interview she claimed that most people "don't know," later she said, "Just about everybody knows. I still have the same friends as before, so. . . ."

Also, her sex change did not take on the same importance to her as it does to so many other transsexuals, who often view it as nothing less than a rebirth. Her relative casualness in this regard became apparent when she was asked about her name change. Here is what she said about that: "My new name? One day the nurse just took down my old name and put up 'Lisa.' It has the same initial so I just kept it."

On the masculinity-femininity scale she appeared less conservative in her endorsement of traditional sex ascriptions than some of the other transsexuals. For example, she did not endorse the double standard of sexual morality and she strongly disagreed with most stereotypical sex ascriptions. Furthermore, she described herself in more masculine stereotypes than any other transsexual. While taking the masculinity-femininity scale she sometimes made comments such as: "I can't stand domineering men!" "I don't agree that men should compete and women should cooperate. It all depends on the situation!" "That's a lot of bullshit, that men shouldn't worry about being young and attractive!"

In sum, Lisa did not fit the housewife model in terms of her attitudes, appearance and lifestyle. Quite to the contrary, the type of postoperative adjustment she was making involved a certain indifference towards middle-class standards of morality and behavior, an emphasis on the sexual aspects of the conversion operation, and a career in show business. Hence Lisa was not truly passing. From a former female impersonator, she had become a sex-change nightclub entertainer, still circulating in the same milieu. The physical conversion had resulted in little *sociological* change.

Here, then, is the showbusiness type of adjustment. None of these transsexuals was married, and all were nightclub performers, with the possible exception of Bobbie, who was a full-time prostitute. All were strippers except Lisa, whose act was mostly singing and comedy. Some were old, heavy set, masculine and low-voiced, thus unlikely to ever pass as natural-born females. Others were younger, more attractive and more feminine than any of the housewife types. Therefore, a nightclub career seems to have been selected not only by those unable to land a husband, but also by those to whom the financial exploitation of their feminine physiques appeared most promising. Ceteris paribus, those who had already been in the business as female impersonators prior to their operations were more likely to become showbusiness types afterwards.

While the stripper type and the housewife type represent the two most clearly contrasting modes of postoperative adjustment, a number of transsexuals did not fit either type. To best describe those individuals, it had to be kept in mind that some feminized transsexuals tend, at least temperamentally, toward the housewife while not (yet) having achieved that status, and that some among them are becoming determined career women, but not in the seamy regions of show business. To deal with these further possibilities, two additional types are presented: the aspiring housewife and the career woman.

Sylvia: The Aspiring Housewife

Only four transsexuals were actually married, but the values embodied by the housewife type were shared by many other transsexuals, in fact by most of them. We saw that even strippers like Renee and Lisa pay at least lip service to conservative standards of sexual morality. Thus many transsexuals seem to be at least *aspiring* housewives.

One group of transsexuals, while not married, shared with the housewives not only ambitions of monogamous respectability and middle-class domesticity, but also — unlike the strippers — a fairly straight occupational and social life. The respondents most typical of this category combined a masculine appearance with a certain inadequacy as females, sometimes due to surgical complications. It may be that their failure to have thus far achieved their housewifely objectives is related to those physical limitations.

Sylvia was typical of this group. She was a shy, quiet woman of thirty-five. She was somewhat large and heavy, but looked younger than her age. She still wore braces around one leg due to temporary paralysis resulting from the operation. Her long red hair was tied up elegantly in a knot. Her voice was soft and feminine. During our first interview, in my office, she told me that she was born in rural South Dakota, where she spent most of her life on the farm, moving to the Twin Cities in 1960. Her father is a retired farmer. She has always been, and still is, a practicing Roman Catholic, something that may be kept in mind when we see, momentarily, how conservative and even puritanic Sylvia's sexual morality is. She is now a secretary at a Catholic institution in the Twin Cities, a new job she assumed after her conversion operation. She has completed high school. She has not been married. She had surgery in March 1968, and has had to come back four times for corrective surgery.

I first asked Sylvia some questions about her background, schooling, her jobs and family. At first she seemed reluctant to talk, answering most questions with a simple yes or no, with a slight smile sometimes, or laughter or a giggle, but very few comments. Later on she unwound. Here is how it went.

"What do you do at the present time?" I asked.

"The same work as before, secretary . . . but I get less now than I made before. . . ."

"Is this the same job?"

"No, it's a different job. I'm secretary to a nun at Saint. . . ."
"Were you living in the Twin Cities before?"
"Yes."
"How has your family reacted to your sex conversion?"
"Well, everyone in the family accepts it except my father. He doesn't at all. He doesn't want to have anything to do with me at all."
"Have you been back to South Dakota?" (her home)
"No, I haven't."
"When was your operation?"
"In March 1968."
"And you haven't been back since? Have you seen any of them?"
"No, I haven't seen them, not even my mother. . . ."
"How about your brothers and sisters?"
"I have two sisters. I am in contact with them, letters, telephone. But the family doesn't want me to come back. . . ."
"Does that bother you?"
"Oh yes. . . ." she said, very sadly.

*   *   *   *

"Well, what made you decide to go through with the operation?"
"I'd always wanted to do it, and the only problem had been financial. This didn't cost me anything. . . . By 'always' I mean ever since I found it could be done . . . I know it was sort of an unrealistic dream!"
"Did you date boys, or girls before?"
"Only boys . . . I had a real bad time in high school. I was quite effeminate. It was quite obvious I guess to everyone. I moved to the Twin Cities in 1960."
"Did things improve then?"
"Well, in ways it was better living here and in ways it was about the same. Living in a small town was very difficult."
"Now what would you say was the main difference between you and other men like you, before your surgery?"
"Well, mentally I always thought of myself as a woman, even

when I was young. I don't even remember ever thinking of myself as a man. Evidently I appeared to people to be feminine although I didn't realize it at the time . . . well I did too, but I wasn't *trying*, if you understand. . . . I never participated in sports, but I didn't have any difficulty before I started high school. I mean before this undoubtedly people noticed it but they didn't make a point of it, it didn't seem to upset anyone, then I started high school and then people noticed it more I guess."

"How has the sex change affected your life?"

"Well, it's somewhat easier to live [laugh]. When you walk down the street, no one notices that you are unusual . . . this is a big thing in itself. But there are lots of problems. Because my surgery did not change the outside world. It takes a woman a long time to become a real woman; to get the maturity, the adulthood. You can't accomplish everything in one year – the social adjustment, the personal adjustment."

"Did you dress as a woman before?"

"Sometimes, not always. I didn't work as a woman."

"What were the main problems with the operation. Obviously there must have been some complications, or else you wouldn't be wearing leg braces."

"Oh, I had lots of problems. I had four surgeries and one was a very serious one. I am still healing. They said last October that it would take about a year to heal. They did a real sloppy job! I don't understand why; they had all the experience with the other ones before me! They were negligent! You could be there and die and they wouldn't do anything! My vagina functions beautifully but it doesn't look like the real thing, it looks terrible! Because of my leg braces I'm temporarily handicapped. You'd think they would have perfected their surgery technqiue after all this time. Five months in the hospital has drastically changed my mind; I wouldn't recommend this operation lightly!"

I asked Sylvia whether she therefore regretted having had the conversion operation.

She backtracked and said, "Well, it's too early to tell . . . I've always been a woman, even before the operation. . . . Anyway the doctors say that I'll be among the most successful transsexuals; I have the best chances for excellent adjustment as a woman. . . ."

"Ultimately, what makes the difference between a man and a woman?"

"Probably the ability to behave like a woman. Before I felt like a woman, and if I behaved like a woman it was noticeable and nonacceptable, whereas now it's acceptable. In fact a woman can behave in almost any way and it's acceptable, I mean respectable. There isn't as much emphasis put on how a woman acts as there is on how a man acts. A man must act slightly masculine. If a woman acts masculine, people don't notice it as much as they do if a man acts feminine."

"Do most people around you know that you are a sex change?"

"Most people don't know. Only my family, the doctors, some friends know, that's all. Nobody that I work with at Saint . . . knows. . . ."

"Who are your present friends?"

"My close friends? Some of them are homosexuals, some are transsexuals, some are straight. At work, the closest ones are a couple of other secretaries. Also Lisa, one of the first ones to have surgery. . . . She was very helpful, even before she had had her operation. We had talked, she had plans to have it somewhere else and she wanted me to come along. . . . Another new friend, surprisingly, is a friend's aunt who I didn't know real well. . . . When I was in the hospital I got a real nice letter from her and she just wasn't the type that you'd think you'd hear from her. In that letter she said she thought this was the right thing to do, *etc*. . . .

"Another friend is Roberta, she is older, I don't think you'd ever get her real age out of her. She is a private patient who just had surgery, not one on the program. I knew her before, and she was always encouraging and helpful. . . . I know several transsexuals who are trying to get surgery elsewhere . . . anyway they can get it!"

"Do you feel any conflicts between your family and some of your transsexual friends?"

"No, because I just don't associate with my family anymore. There are no demands from my family. They don't know any of my present friends."

"You changed jobs after your operation. Why?"

"Mostly because I just couldn't . . . I didn't exactly know how to tell my former boss. And afterwards I found out that if I had told him it would have made no difference . . . he knows now. I talked to him on the telephone, because I worked there for six years and I wanted to use it as a reference for getting a new job and he said that if he had an opening I'd be welcome to come back . . . I'm not planning to move."

"How many jobs have you had since your conversion operation?"

"Two. I was working at a place before my surgery, that I stayed at. I had only been there for about six months. Then I changed to this one."

"Did those people know?" (first job)

"Well, I didn't think they did, but then they found out. . . ."

"How was it received?"

"Okay . . . well, it was a company that dealt with homosexual merchandise. . . . On my new job nobody knows."

"Who would you now be most reluctant to disclose your sex conversion to?"

"Probably the people at work."

"Would you tell your husband?"

"Yes."

What transpired from Sylvia's responses was a highly "straight," concealed and "reformed" approach to life and sexuality. For one thing, we saw that the majority of her new acquaintances do not know that she is a sex change. Thus, while she does have several transsexuals among her friends, she is truly in the process of passing. Furthermore, not only is she gainfully employed rather than being a housewife, but it is as a secretary for a nun at a Catholic institution. A far cry from the favorite alternative occupation among transsexuals, nightclub stripping!

Also, the masculinity-femininity scale revealed what Sylvia's attitudes were truly like. She strongly disagreed with the double standard of sexual morality, but only because she was opposed to extramarital sex for *both* men and women! In general, she agreed with a large number of stereotypical sex ascriptions, and when she talked about herself, it was mostly in feminine terms.

Discussing her reading preferences, she said, ". . . I like fashion magazines like *Vogue* and *McCalls*. . . . I am quite familiar with some confession magazines. . . . As far as books are concerned, well, I didn't like *Myra Breckenridge.* I didn't like this other book written by a sex change either. The title of it was *I Was a Man.* That's such a ridiculous idea, 'I was a man'!' "

When asked how she felt about engagement and wedding, she replied, "Engagement isn't too important . . . I have been engaged before. But a wedding ring is!'' (laughs)

Thus Sylvia was clearly an aspiring housewife. Her morality was that of a prudish young woman, reflecting her rural, Catholic upbringing. No doubt the fact that she has steered clear of a stripping career is related to the fact that she has never been involved in nightlife showbusiness. Unlike many other transsexuals, she was not a female impersonator before her operation. She did cross-dress, but only privately. Marriage is her eventual goal and meanwhile, as a secretary to a nun, her life is aimed at the establishment of respectability. This involves a gradual passage into full-fledged womanhood, and thus, Sylvia quit a job where people knew, in favor of one where they did not. Also, her opinion that the ultimate criterion of womanhood is "being accepted as a woman," and not necessarily physiological, indicates Sylvia's emphasis on social acceptability rather than the mere sexual.

On one occasion I interviewed Sylvia and another transsexual, Jane, simultaneously. This led to some interesting disagreements between these two respondents which highlight the differences between an aspiring housewife (Sylvia) and a stripper (Jane).

Jane was a thirty-two-year-old blonde — petite and heavily made up. She was friendly and more outgoing than Sylvia. When she arrived at the hospital offices for the interview, she was in a disheveled state, her short hair tangled up, and carrying a pungent alcoholic smell. The first impression, then, was one of poor postoperative adjustment. This was corroborated when some hospital personnel told me that Jane had come drunk to several earlier appointments with doctors and psychiatrists, and that she had emotional problems and a drinking problem.

She was born and raised in rural Minnesota, coming from a lower-class Lutheran family. Her father was a laborer. She did not finish high school and lived in her home town for most of her life, the exception being a three-year stay in a state mental institution. She underwent the sex conversion operation early in 1968 and came back for corrective surgery about half a year later. She has never been married, worked now in a nightclub and was also probably a prostitute. Jane's social life was as disjointed as that of most other transsexuals.

Concerning her family, here is some of what she had to say: ". . . I don't get along with my parents, and yet I want to. I want to make a better life for myself so they'll accept me, but my boyfriend and them never get along. I pay more attention to my boyfriend than to them . . . he owns two businesses, he has several trucks and drivers for him. . . . But my friends and my family never get along. . . . Most of my friends are males or transsexuals, so you can imagine how my folks feel about them. . . . My father had me committed for three years when I was eighteen. He wouldn't let me out till the doctors put the pressure on him. Dr. . . . finally got me out of the mental hospital. My father named me . . . after a famous baseball player." (She laughs at the apparent absurdity of such an expectation.)

The most interesting part of this interview occurred when Jane and Sylvia disagreed on the issue of passing. I had already asked Sylvia how many people knew that she was a sex change. She said, "Only my best friends, my family and the doctors."

To the question whether she ever voluntarily divulges her sex change to anyone, she replied: "Only if I am going with somebody and I feel I should tell rather than have him hear it from someone else."

I then asked Jane the same questions. Her reply: "Well, a lot of people know. . . . Of course I don't go around telling strangers about it. . . ."

"How about if you get married? Will you tell your husband and children?"

"Yes, I would have to. . . . If the children were older and the kids at school were talking about it and one of my children came home and said 'Mom, the kids at school say you're not really my mom,' well I would have to tell them, wouldn't I?"

"No!" said Sylvia emphatically. "I would never tell them. I

would move out of the state so no one knows."

"But the chances of them finding out are too great," Jane replied. "You're better off telling them. If they love you it'll be alright anyway."

"That depends on the child," Sylvia persisted. "If I had adopted very young children I would just move as far as possible so they'd never find out."

"Well, chances are we'll never be allowed to adopt children anyway; our background doesn't recommend us very well!"

"I don't agree!" Sylvia interrupted. "My greatest ambition is to have children before I'm old!"

Thus, Sylvia and Jane had entirely different views as to the best possible type of adjustment. One definitely aimed at middle-class femininity, the other had more or less given up on that.

Most transsexuals made statements suggesting at least some dissatisfaction with being an overt transsexual, with being in underworld showbusiness, with deviant sexuality, and with deviance in general. Ultimately, all transsexuals undertake their feminization process, both surgical and social-psychological, for two reasons: (a) to realize their life-long ambitions to become women, and (b) to gain greater social acceptance and respectability than they enjoyed prior to their operations, as homosexuals, transvestites, or some other category of social outcasts. Hence, while many transsexuals once again land in marginal roles after their operations (stripping, prostitution, *etc.*), these roles are somewhat more acceptable, both to them and to middle-class society. The general trend that accompanies feminization is one towards greater middle-class acceptability. All transsexuals are consciously engaged in this developmental effort, an effort not pursued with equal vigor or success by all, but which logically extends to the role of suburban-housewife-with-children.

Vanessa: The Career Woman

Thus far we have distinguished between transsexuals who aim for middle-class respectability and transsexuals who work in seamy areas of entertainment. Yet it would be wrong to conclude that only two options are available to transsexuals — housewife respectability, or financial success at the cost of privacy and respectability. An important additional category, then, is that of the "respectable" career woman. This is the transsexual who neither embraces roles of domesticity nor makes a living by somehow selling herself sexually or as a freak. This transsexual is gainfully employed and career oriented, but as a businesswoman, a scientist or a writer, and not necessarily in showbusiness, publicizing her sex change or stripping in a nightclub. In sum, this is the transsexual who aims *both* at status passage *and* a career, hoping to reconcile middle-class respectability and work.

Most typical of this category was Vanessa, the only Ph.D. in the sample, who worked both before and after her sex conversion as a scientific consultant for a major Twin Cities firm. I first interviewed Vanessa at her home, where she was still bedridden and recovering from her operation which had taken place only two weeks earlier, the latest one in the project. The ravages of very recent sex surgery were still apparent, and a contributing factor was Vanessa's age. At forty-five, she was among the oldest transsexuals in the project. As I observed her, she was in bad need of a shave, and her cranial hair had partly fallen out, possibly in relation to hormonal complications. Her voice was low and her Adam's apple was protruding; her body was muscular and angular. It was difficult to predict whether she would eventually do a better job at "being a woman."

It was therefore rather surprising to see her, as she came to my office for another interview a month later, blossomed into a fairly attractive and extremely vigorous individual. She now wore an expensive silky dress, a tall blonde wig and heavy make-up. During the interview I learned that Vanessa was born in a large Southern city from middle-class Catholic parents. She graduated with a B.B.A. from an excellent university and moved North where she began to climb up the executive ladder in a large Minneapolis coporation. She then went on to receive a Ph.D. in psychology, and became a research consultant for the firm.

While in college, twenty-five years ago, she married a woman by the name of Rose, and they had a girl who is now a nineteen-year-old college coed. Roberta's transvestite practices while married were known and tolerated by Rose. The couple became divorced two years before Roberta's sex change.

Her university training and long professional experience became apparent during the interview. She was very intelligent, well-read and well-informed. We spent some time discussing Ayn Rand's *Objectivism* and her appraisal of her own pathology showed a sophisticated grasp of clinical psychology. She seemed eager to cooperate with the research and delighted with her sex conversion. I began by asking her how she felt.

Her answer: "Great! All of a sudden I want tommorrow, I want some more time. You see, I started later than most people! Money is also important. . . . But I wouldn't want to be that kind of a feminine female that I'd lose all my former identity. The idea of 'me' is important."

"How did the transition go?"

"I was being schizophrenic, like in *Three Faces of Eve*. I didn't know who I was in the morning when I got up, whether I was John or Vanessa. This lasted for about a month. At the end of a month there was no John left, only a sense of relief. In other words I suffered from a month-long psychotic episode. . . . I've always wanted to go through with this. . . . John is somebody that's gone away, that I remember very nicely. Somebody very friendly . . . but he isn't dead! I am still very fond of him. . . . I may not have turned out to be Miss Femininity herself, but that was to be expected. My deep voice doesn't bother me anymore; I found out that people find a deep voice sexy, anyway. I also have a very heavy beard, it grows as much as before, but some women have as much facial hair as I do. . . ."

"What was your main reason for requesting the operation?"

"It's the psychological thing . . . I need the reassurance that I am a woman. I don't have a man to make love to me, and I don't care . . . besides I'm kind of scared anyway."

I asked Vanessa some standard background questions, first about her education.

Her answers: "Well, I am a high school dropout, but at twenty I enrolled at the University. I have a B.A. in Business Administration and a Ph.D. in psychology."

"What is your religion originally?"

"I believe the family was Roman Catholic, but I think most of the relatives are free thinkers. As I recall there is a whole mixture of religions in the family. . . ."

"What is your age?"

"Forty-five. I should say thirty-three, that's nobody's true age."

"Have you been married?"

"Yes . . . you mean my marriage to a female at one point?"

"What happened?"

"Well, I'd been going with Rose during college years as a date, and I'd been living with Fritz previous to the age of twenty-one, and it was under his influence that I went to college and then after that he sort of urged me that I wouldn't get ahead as a young male unless I was married, and we were. . . ."

"How long did it last?"

"Oh, too long [laughs], well I don't mean that . . . twenty-five years. There is one child . . . after that child came I felt trapped in the marriage, so I think I made out the best I could. The marriage eventually developed into a brother-sister relationship. It never was a very strong sexual union as I recall. In the five years before marriage I think I only had sex with Rose once. We became divorced two years ago. There were no hard feelings, I still talk to her and we still have the common interest of the daughter. Of course I don't think you can break up something that lasted twenty-five years without some misgivings on both parts, although Rose, I think, would have just as soon continued with the security of the situation as it existed. She was content with it, as bad as it was for me."

"Why was it bad for you?"

"Well, it's the pretense of being something you are really not; of trying to be male, and operating in a male's world and operate the way a male is expected to operate, being nagged about it a great deal. Those are things that were very uncomfortable. . . . I was always a woman, I wasn't a man. I tried terribly hard to conform to male roles. I tried to survive. I dressed well and neatly, I rarely cross-dressed, I tried to express the distinction between a woman and a man in my appearance. But John looked like a nelly boy. . . ."

"How has your family reacted to the new situation?"

"Well, first there was the divorce. It was a little difficult in coming because there was fairly substantial property involved — I have done fairly well for my wife and my daughter over the years — so it took some doing to negotiate a settlement that would be reasonably fair to all parties involved. . . ."

"How has your daughter reacted to your operation?"

"Well, my daughter was informed of the reason for the divorce and she was shook up quite a bit about it, and somehow or other after our reassurance that it could never happen to her, she sort of accepted it. . . . Now, just recently she called me and I informed her that surgery had occured, because you see this was so recent. . . . I did go into the hospital without letting them know about it, I didn't let any of the family know, on either side, and even my business associates and employers do not know the type of surgery that I had. But my daughter apparently was making inquiries about me not being home. I had been in contact with her at least once or twice weekly since the divorce, by phone or in person, and during this period of surgery she began to wonder where I was. . . . Once I called her from the hospital, but under the pretense that I was calling her from out of town."

"How old is she, by the way?"

"She is nineteen and she is a nursing student. . . . I think she is intelligent and very self-reliant. Anyway, I called up from the hospital and explained the whole story. She listened very carefully, we had a long conversation about it; I asked her to, at least for the present, maintain secrecy just between us, until the appropriate time to advise Rose that surgery took place. . . ."

"Rose doesn't know?"

"As far as I know she doesn't know yet. . . . Well, as far as Paula is concerned [daughter], what brought it to a head is, I was praying for a way to advise her, and then she called me one time and asked me 'Are we going to get together, because remember, 15th is Father's Day.' And I said, 'Paula, of course I love you very much, but I do have to tell you that I can no longer accept Father's Day gifts. If you wish to continue relations with me I could be your special Aunt Vanessa or something like that, but please don't remind me of that situation and certainly don't bring me any male clothing under any circumstances.' "

"Did your wife and daughter know that you were cross-dressing before the operation?"

"Yes, my wife knew of cross-dressing and my daughter knew of it too, because my wife had told her and showed her pictures, although my daughter had never actually seen me that I know of. She may have seen me unexpectedly without saying anything about it, because I have done it quite openly, coming and going on weekends so she could very well have seen me, but at no time has she ever indicated that she does know. . . . Now she ended up our conversation saying, nevertheless, 'I'd like to see you,' so I'm looking forward to meeting her, at least for the first time. We have gotten along very well, I've gone shopping with her and it has been more like two females, she would allow me to discuss clothing with her. This happened within the last three years. She has always helped me to pick materials and to pick patterns for clothing. The relationship is not what you would expect between daughter and father. I think it goes a little deeper. I think she senses and appreciates my basic feminine interests in her wardrobe, just like all women are interested."

"How has the rest of your family reacted to your sex change?"

"My family knows about the situation; I understand they had a council, and they decided to leave me alone, so there are no demands made on me. They leave me alone. I have two brothers living here and a sister in Wisconsin. If I choose to visit them I am welcome. Last time I showed up I had fairly long hair and I guess I upset them; I heard about that! I also recently visited my sister in Wisconsin and I had pretty long hair but nevertheless, we had a very interesting conversation and we just talked girl talk, believe it or not. . . .

It's going to be interesting, the surgery is so recent. But I'm sure I won't have any problem of acceptance in the family, they all understand. Apparently they have decided that they should just leave me alone. I have never mentioned that I was going to have surgery beforehand because I felt that would be the same as asking them for a decision, which I have no right to do, but now that the decision has been made by me and by my doctors, then I think it's a different story. . . . The only thing is, they have a little trouble calling me by my new first name; and pronouns, of course, are difficult. There are seven or nine nieces and nephews under eight in the family. They are the ones who correct my parents: 'It's not *he*, it's *she*,' they tell them. 'It's not John anymore, it's Vanessa. . . .'

"The new situation is hardest on my mother. She prefers men. Superficially everyone likes it, but there is partiality towards boys in my family . . . my mother is uncomfortable with me. My father is fine. . . . I have two sisters and one brother, they are all nice to me. The nicest thing my father said was when I told my parents of my plans to go through with it — my mother just sat silently — he said, 'So what's the big deal? You can always come home!' "

"How many people know of your conversion operation, besides your family?"

"At work, of course, everyone knows. They were all told by the chief. Otherwise, I still do business with mostly the same people as before, I still go to the same grocery store, *etc.,* so most people know. I only changed banks. The only trouble is with some of the neighbors. The kids whistle, holler at me, call me names. A lady verbally attacked me . . . of course she was not really a lady . . . but most people I have had contact with are nice. My ex-boss called me to come back to the same job. No one recognized me. I had had long hair before I went cross-dressed. I had planned on changing my whole life, move away, change jobs, *etc.,* but I didn't have to. . . ."

"Do you ever voluntarily disclose your sex change to any-one?"

"Only in business dealings, when I have to, like applying for credit."

Part of the interview dealt with Vanessa's self-concept and gender identity. I first asked her how she felt about the sex change.

She replied, "Very good. I feel such peace of mind, and right now it's just patiently waiting to get my health restored and to get over the pains, but I am so happy about it. I'm looking forward to the future. . . ."

"Have you mistakenly been taken for a member of the opposite sex?"

"Well, as a male I have been taken as a female — voice, you know, on the telephone, and people have said, 'You look like a dike,' even in male clothing. I have been taken as a woman. I have certain masculine characteristics, but I haven't had any response, except with some of the guys that I've been close to. Eventually one might say, when I was resisting his advances, 'Why baby, don't resist,' so he wanted a homosexual relationship."

"Tell me something about your change of name."

"Well, I am kind of choosing these new names because I rather think that my mother wanted a girl when I was born and I think that she had these names picked out as I have."

"Who would you be most reluctant to disclose your true identity to?"

"My feeling is never to disclose it to anyone. If they know, fine; if they don't, I'm not going to say anything. But I would be most reluctant to tell it to a date, I suppose . . . but I think my husband should know, in one form or another."

As far as friends and significant others are concerned, Vanessa said: "I have a pretty good mixture of friends; some are couples, single men, single women. . . . I guess Fritz has been the most important person in my life, and there is Linda, a young girl who just had sex surgery; we have a real close relationship. . . . There have been a number of doctors, too, who were helpful. Dr. . . ., in New York, who was my initial adviser, and brother Bhaktananda, a yogi of a monastic order who has been my spiritual counselor. . . ."

"Who was Fritz?"

"Fritz was someone I had met when I was single, and Fritz asked me to move with him and we lived together for six years before I was married. At the same time I was dating Rose. At his urgings I got married to Rose. We were lifelong friends after that. Fritz was my family you see, because he was a good, true friend and I always felt that I had someone and I always imagined him as my husband, in a sort of a fancy way . . . you know, mental fancy."

"Did your wife know that you were frequenting Fritz?"

"I don't know just what you mean there . . . oh yes, I see. Well, he was a friend of the family, too. There was no sexual relation. I think in the earlier days Fritz attempted homosexual sex with me once or twice or three times. Then I think he had guilt feelings about it and he stopped and he just wouldn't do after that. A sex relationship was not part of our relationship.

"After marriage I moved away but Fritz continued to be a friend of the family, you see. He was my side of the family, just like her mother and her sisters were her family. He was always Uncle Fritz to us. He was my friend all during these years, even though I was perhaps somewhat alone in the world. In terms of acceptance I always felt that I had Fritz for a friend. And of course that makes the years easier to take. I never had any extensive friendships among males, but Fritz was my one friend until he died."

Vanessa's masculinity-femininity scores expressed a greater than average sexual liberalism. Even when she agreed with traditional stereotypes and ascriptions, she often cautiously dissociated herself from them, as in the following two instances: "It's true that men should win over women in competitive situations. But only because it's better for their ego." And: "Confession magazines? For women exclusively. I like the stories, even though it's trash. . . ."

Thus Vanessa was too well educated to blindly endorse the conservative attitudes most typical of the housewives. However, she was not planning on a career of loose morality either. That she may be appropriately labeled a career woman became apparent when the interview moved on to deal with her occupational milieu and aspirations. It went as follows:

"What is your job?"

"I am a research scientist with. . . ."

"Is this the same position as prior to surgery?"

"Yes."

"Were there difficulties in going back to this same position? Did you find lack of acceptance as a new female?"

"Well, I had only worked there as a male. So I discussed this going back to work with some people at. . . . They looked at it favorably, they said that I seem to have the mischievousness to want to go back in the first place, not to fear it. I didn't fear going back, I welcomed the idea. I have a large office, there are thirty people in the office that work under me and it was quite interesting to see how many people thought of this as a nut house, and how many people were accepting. I expected to walk in unconcernedly, and that's it! But I had to get some help of a psychiatrist to discuss this with him — we have a psychologist on the payroll.

"Anyway, most of my immediate associates have been very decent about it; there is of course a small number of people that are extremely prejudiced. To them this concept of male and female are the only acceptable, and all forms of deviation are just absolutely anathema, but most people couldn't care less. They are tolerant and understanding of my problems. They judge me like they would judge any other individual. . . .

"It is very interesting in connection with my job, though, I was advised that I would never be selected to be promoted to treasurer. The reason was expressed so awkwardly; they didn't say it was 'because of your sex change' but because 'of the way you communicate.' And the psychologist has repeated the same thing. . . . So I suppose they have a little ill feeling toward me, but on the other hand, knowing ultimately what happened they understand it better. . . .As one of the principal consultants to the organization I should have made appearances before farmers but they never let me make speaking appearances. When my boss quit, they replaced him with a man from out of town. They appointed a younger man than I, a man who had been in the organization fewer years than I was, as a treasurer. They appointed him over me. It caused me no distress whatsoever because I know what it is all about. The treasurer must negotiate with government agencies, with customers, with other groups in the dairy industry, and it is a high level occupation. They said 'you may be technically very well qualified to handle a job like that, but because of the way you communicate . . .,' so they couldn't select me for the job. But a woman could very well operate as a research consultant in the role that I have operated in; it is in the nature of a service job."

Apparently Vanessa's future plans depended much on developments on the job, in the organization. Her sex change had converted her from a married house-father into a single woman, but one thing she expected to remain unchanged: her important position with the company, i.e. her career. She had a competitive business attitude not found among the housewives. The main focus of her life was in the competitive business world. As she said: "I always compete, with men as well as women. In fact, I have even been blackmailed. It happened once before the operation. Some people were very jealous, they didn't like me and wanted my place, so they were going to go to my boss and tell him that I was planning to get a sex change operation. . . ."

The overall impression made by Vanessa was that of an active and intellectual individual, far removed from the underworld sexuality of so many other transsexuals. As indicated, her masculinity-femininity scores were quite liberal. That is, she did not subscribe to the current nature of the division of labor (for example, she strongly disagreed that teaching is mostly for women), and to such stereotypes as the competitive male and the supportive female. This may be a function of her high education. In addition, she viewed herself as only partially female, even after the operation. As she phrased it, "the idea of 'me' is important," indicating a need for continuity in her identity. Thus, Vanessa was the rare transsexual who did not see the desirability of total passage into the status of natural-born female and of a total break with the past. She acknowledged the importance of money, but this did not mean that she chose to exhibit herself to the public as a transsexual. She did not actively steer toward marriage and middle-class domesticity, but neither was she on a sexual fling. She was a dedicated career woman.

This chapter has presented four types of postoperative adjustment. First the housewife type was portrayed; a type representing mostly transsexuals who marry and settle down in a middle-class lifestyle as soon as possible after their conversion. This was Sally. Of course, additional transsexuals share the values and ambitions of the housewives and several can be expected to join their ranks in the future. Next, the showbusiness type or the stripper type, was presented. These are the transsexuals who care the least about marriage, domesticity and middle-class respectability, and who choose instead to exploit their newly acquired femininity by tripping or stripping, working in nightclubs, practising prostitution, or exhibiting themselves as transsexuals to the public. Renee and Lisa represent this type, the former being an exquisitely attractive young stripper, the latter more of a grotesque freak. The housewife type and the showbusiness type represent the two most contrasting modes of postoperative adjustment.

Two additional types of feminized transsexuals were discerned. The aspiring housewife is a transsexual who shares the married housewife's goal and values, but who for some reason has not been able to actualize these goals. The reason that these transsexuals have remained mere aspiring housewives may have to do with their less than satisfactory physical feminization. Indeed, Sylvia, the model for this form of adjustment, was depicted as a less than attractive and feminine transsexual. It may also be that these transsexuals have artificial vaginas that do not function adequately.

Finally, the fourth type that was discerned was that of the career woman, representing transsexuals who do not necessarily view marital domesticity as the ultimate fulfillment of the true woman, but who neither descend into prostitution and striptease as a way of life. These transsexuals are gainfully employed, but in such "respectable" fields as business, research and writing. The case material portraying Vanessa was reproduced here as being illustrative of this type.

It should be kept in mind that in all four types, material was derived from many different transsexuals, representing composit portraits. In the final analysis, no transsexual can be described entirely in terms of one type of adjustment. All transsexuals share certain middle-class ambitions as well as exhibitionistic tendencies. All wish to marry and all are to some extent sexual deviants. All of them would like to pass and all see financial and other benefits in publicizing their sex change. There are, however, differences in emphasis and it is on that basis that the four types have been formulated.

Chapter 4

$\bigl($ TO PASS OR NOT TO PASS $\bigr)$

F_{OUR} types of transsexuals have been discerned: the housewife type, the stripper, the aspiring housewife and the career woman. These types embody modes of social adjustment that differ along a vast number of variables, including marital status, occupation, status passage and goals. In addition, the following variables are concomitants or perhaps causal factors of postoperative patterns of adjustment: physical appearance, physical outcome of the sex surgery, past history of homosexuality, transvestism and nightclub participation, demographic background, length of time since the surgery, age, motives for having undergone the sex change and ways of dealing with the stigma. This chapter deals with these variables and relates them to passing.

The Passers and the Nonpassers

The single most salient dimension along which transsexuals differ is "respectability." That is, while all transsexuals undergo sex change because they wish to be fullfledged women, they do not all strive with equal zeal toward "respectable" womanhood. Now the three factors that are most crucial to the transsexual in making up respectable womanhood are marriage, nonemployment and passing. Other things being equal, the married transsexual is a "better woman" than the single transsexual; the domestic transsexual feels that she is better than the career transsexual; finally, the transsexual who passes frequently as a natural-born female is a better woman than the transsexual who does not pass.

Status passage is the most fundamental sociological concept that may be applied to the transsexual experience. All individuals in society undergo various status passages during their lives

(Becker and Strauss; Strauss). This occurs for example when a woman passes from single to married status, when a man passes from civilian to military status or when a college graduate passes from the status of student to a professional status. Thus men and women occupy a variety of statuses and pass into various positions that may be either achieved or ascribed to them (Linton). When such status passage is fraudulent, it is called *passing*. Passing may be seen as fraudulent status passage, because it is the type of passage in which the individual conceals his former status(es). A police officer with a criminal record may be said to be passing if his record is not currently known to his peers and his superiors. A classical example of passing is provided by the light-skinned Negro who passes as a dark-skinned Caucasian (Myrdal). However, biological factors, inborn or acquired, are generally more difficult to conceal than biographical information, so that passing is rare when it comes to moving between statuses that are physically rooted.

One inborn biological factor that seems so inescapable as to make passing virtually impossible is sex. Yet transsexuals represent a category of people who have not only undertaken a status passage hitherto hardly conceivable, namely sexual passage, but in addition, some are passing. That is, some feminized transsexuals often conceal the fact that they were ever male. Such is the case of Sally, whose own husband does not know!

Passing always entails the risks of unintended disclosure and consequent sanctions. To offset these risks, the major rewards that passing must offer are generally by way of greater social acceptance, primarily acceptance by one's favored reference groups. It is therefore generally the deviant, the minority member and the social alienate who seek to pass so as to become accepted by more dominant or respectable groups. In some form or another, the status that one relinquishes and conceals bears stigma, at least in the eyes of the group one is attempting to join.*

---

*Of course, passing is not always a case of the deviant attempting to establish "normal" or respectable identity. The new recruit to the counterculture may wish to conceal from his peers his upper middle-class origin and his B.A. in accounting. Here, the counterculture is the positive reference group, while former affiliation with the ➤

Goffman (1963) distinguished between stigma that is discredited and stigma that is discreditable. The former occurs when an individual's stigma is perceived and known to others, for example in the face to face interactions of the visibly handicapped, overt homosexuals, minority members and known criminals. On the other hand, stigma is merely discreditable when it is presumably known only to its possessor. Examples of this are provided by the covert homosexual, the exconvict or the former mental patient who are not known in their current milieu to have a record, or any other interaction in which passing occurs.

Transsexualism is a stigma that may be both discredited and discreditable. In fact the same transsexual often experiences situations in which her stigma is known, and situations where it is not. In the latter case, she is passing as a natural-born female.

The greater a transsexual's tendency is to pass, the more closely she approximates her vision of respectable womanhood. It is essentially this respectability dimension that served as a basis for the typology established in the preceding chapter. When distinguishing between the housewife type, the aspiring housewife, the career woman and the stripper type, the three factors singled out as most frequently used by transsexuals to establish respectability were marriage, domestic roles and passing as natural-born females. Because marriage is a possibility of which more transsexuals may take advantage in the future, the typology focused primarily on the two other components of respectability: domesticity and passing. It can now be shown that the four types of transsexuals emerged out of the intersection of these two dimensions, as becomes clear from Table V.

In Table V, one could assign a high respectability score to those transsexuals who play predominantly domestic roles and a low one to those who play professional roles, for example 2 and 1, respectively. Similarly one could assign a score of 2 to transsexuals who tend to pass and a score of 1 to those who do not, indicating,

---

establishment provides the blemish that must be washed off. Neither is passing always motivated by considerations of social acceptance. Griffin (1960), who spent a period of time in the southern United States passing as a Negro did that primarily to obtain information about the American Negro experience which is not available to the white man. Intelligence is, of course, also the objective of the undercover agent.

Table V

A TYPOLOGY OF TRANSSEXUALS

	Pass mostly as natural-born females	Do not often pass as natural-born females
Play predominantly domestic roles	HOUSEWIVES	ASPIRING HOUSEWIVES
Play professional roles		CAREER WOMEN STRIPPERS

respectively, high and low degrees of respectability along that dimension. The resulting respectability scores would be as follows:

Housewives:	4 points
Aspiring Housewives:	3 points
Career Women:	1.5 points
Strippers:	1 point

The meaning of this little game is simply to show that it is possible to view the four types of transsexuals as forming a continuum along respectability, a continuum on which housewives rank highest and strippers lowest.

Of the two factors that make up respectability in this analysis, one is more fundamental than the other. Occupational status, like marital status, is subject to change and must be viewed as an indicator of the transsexual's orientation rather than the embodiment of that orientation.

However, passing is a more general process that may represent the transsexual's overall way of living. The ultimate question for the transsexual, as for many stigmatized minorities, is whether to pass or not to pass. While all transsexuals have relatives who know that they were born biological males, and all presumably sometimes find themselves in public places where they are recognized as mere anonymous women, some are more likely to work at becoming covert sex changes than others.

In order to discern some essential differences between at least two types of transsexuals, we separated the passers from the nonpassers on the basis of the following question: *How many people know of your conversion operation and the fact that until recently you were biologically male?*

Of those who answered the question, seven gave responses that boil down to the fact that "just about everybody knows," while ten said that only a limited number of people know. Table VI gives the breakdown of the sample along this line.

It may be noted that most passers are housewives (Sally) or aspiring housewives (Sylvia), while most nonpassers are strippers (Lisa, Renee, Jane). This is as expected. However, the overlap is not total, two strippers being among the passers (Linda and Joan) and one housewife being among the nonpassers (Adelaide).

A typical passer is Patricia, an aspiring housewife, who said, ". . . Only my best friends, my family and the doctors know. . . . I would tell my husband perhaps, but not to my children. . . . I would move out of the state so no one knows!"

A typical nonpasser is Maryjo, a stripper. As she said, "Everybody knows, at work. When someone keeps questioning me there is no point in me pretending and trying to lie. . . . If I ever got married my husband and my children would have to know or else I couldn't live with him."

Table VI

"HOW MANY PEOPLE KNOW OF YOUR CONVERSION OPERATION AND THE FACT THAT UNTIL RECENTLY YOU WERE A BIOLOGICAL MALE?"

Only a limited number of people know (the passers)	*Just about everybody knows (the nonpassers)*
Sally	Adelaide
Elinor	Elizabeth
Patricia	Lisa
Linda	Maryjo
Vanessa	Renee
Lois	Becky
Sylvia	Jane
Roberta	
Lee	
Joan	
Total 10	7

Variables Related to Passing

Length of Time Since Sex Surgery

Sally was one of the first transsexuals to have undergone the conversion operation at the University of Minnesota, two years ago. She was also the one patient who had managed to pass to such an extent that not even her own husband knew. This led to the hypothesis that passing may be the wave of the future for transsexuals. Does Sally perhaps presage a general trend among transsexuals? Do transsexuals in time tend more and more to pass, to the point where they eventually will not disclose their sex conversion to anyone? In order to test this hypothesis, the average length of time that has lapsed since the initial sex surgery was computed for the passers and the nonpassers. Table VII presents the results.

Table VII reveals that the passers have generally been feminized earlier than the nonpassers. This may indeed indicate that in time more transsexuals will pass.

That passing may occur more and more with time is indicated by the following statements. Sylvia, the self-effacing secretary to a Catholic nun, who underwent surgery over a year prior to our interview and who is now predominatly a passer, said, "Most people [now] don't know. Nobody that I work with at Saint . . . knows. . . . My first job after the operation, they did know!"

Adelaide, on the other hand, had been operated on only three months ago. Her appearance and mannerisms seemed somewhat odd, something that time and further training might perhaps

Table VII

LENGTH OF TIME SINCE SEX CONVERSION OPERATION, RELATED TO PASSING

	The passers (Known to most people as natural-born females)	The nonpassers (Known to most people as transsexuals)
Average length of time since operation (at time of interview)	11 months	8 months

remedy. Adelaide can best be classified as a career woman, and she is a nonpasser. She said, ". . . I wouldn't want to be that kind of a feminine female that I'd lose all my former identity. . . . At work everyone knows. . . ."

Physical Appearance, Physical Outcome of Surgery and Gender Misidentification

A further variable that could be expected to correlate with passing was the physiological aspect of the sex change itself. It would have been possible to use subjective judgment to report on the physical attractiveness of the various transsexuals as women, the expectation being that there would be more good-looking transsexuals among passers than among nonpassers. Instead, a simple scale was used to cover the most salient aspects of the physiological feminization process. These were:

1. Complexion (amount and visibility of facial hair)
2. Voice pitch
3. Breast size
4. Size of Adam's apple
5. Size of calf muscles
6. Overall physical size
7. Femininity of mannerisms
8. Overall attractiveness as a female
9. Functioning vagina

Each subject was given a composite "physical femininity score" that could range from a maximum of nine for high femininity to a minimum of zero for low femininity. The average scores of passers and nonpassers were computed. Figure VIII presents the results.

Table VIII

AVERAGE PHYSICAL FEMININITY SCORES OF PASSERS AND NONPASSERS

High Feminity	The Passers	The Nonpassers	Low Femininity
9	5.50	3.25	0

Figure VIII indicates that the passers tend indeed to have higher physical femininity scores than the nonpassing transsexuals. In plain language, transsexuals who have become good-looking women are more likely to pass than those whose surgical and hormonal feminization has been less successful.

Since the passers are generally the more feminine and the better-looking transsexuals, it could be expected that they would be less frequently misidentified in their gender than the nonpassers. To test this, the transsexuals were asked if, and how often, they are taken for members of the opposite sex.

The responses revealed that misidentification of the nonpassers' sex is indeed more frequent than that of the passers'. A typical passer who claims never to be misidentified is Elinor. Elinor, married now and embracing the housewife model, said, "I never get identified as a member of the opposite sex. Even before the operation I was always identified as a woman. I went dressed as a woman, used women's facilities. . . ."

And indeed, Elinor has a soft and feminine voice, little facial hair and little need to wear heavy make-up.

Lisa, on the other hand, is the very large, heavy-set fifty-year-old feminized transsexual. Her voice is a baritone. Consequently she admits to being frequently taken for a man. In her own words: ". . . yes, it happens several times a day, on the telephone mostly. . . ."

Predictably, Lisa follows the showbusiness model, working in a nightclub in the East.

Most frequently, sexual misidentification is the result of a masculine voice. Maryjo for example has had the same experience as Lisa. When asked whether anyone ever takes her for a man, she replied, "On the phone sometimes, when my voice is low, they say, 'yes sir'." Maryjo, too, has chosen the nightclub route rather than the happily-married-housewife syndrome.

Age

It could also be expected that the passers would generally be younger than the nonpassers. Phrased differently, the younger a transsexual is at the time of her feminization, the better her chances are for total passage into the status of natural-born female. Youth may be expected to work to the transsexual's advantage in two ways: First, the earlier the surgical feminization, the easier the socialization into basic sex roles and feminine mannerisms and etiquette. Secondly, the younger the patient is at the time of her sex conversion, the better-looking a female she becomes. Table IX reproduces the average age of passers and nonpassers.

Transsexuals themselves are aware of the importance of age. Elinor was a passer, twenty-one, and the youngest transsexual of the entire sample. She realized her advantage in this respect, saying: "The doctors say that I will be among the most successful transsexuals. I have the best chances for excellent adjustment as a woman because I am so young."

Lisa, on the other hand, was a nonpasser of fifty, quite aware of her limitations as a result of age. As she saw it: "My operation is not successful . . . I'm too old . . . I'm not as young as the rest of them!"

Geographical Mobility

Perhaps the most frequent concomitant of passing is geographical mobility. What better way is there to be reborn in an entirely new capacity, to go underground, incognito, than to move as far away as possible to a remote city, land or milieu that is beyond the probable reach of one's former associates? In this context, transsexuals were asked the following question: *After you went through your conversion operation, did you move, and if so, how far?*

A tabulation of the answers showed a slightly higher proportion of passers than nonpassers moving. In addition, the passers had

Table IX

AVERAGE AGE OF PASSING AND NONPASSING TRANSSEXUALS

The Passers	*The Nonpassers*
30 years	32 years

moved farther than the nonpassers. Thus the data express a slight relationship between passing and geographical mobility.

It may be recalled that several transsexuals, while considering moving, had not yet done so. That geographical mobility is clearly related to passing in some cases is evidenced by Lisa who, having moved to the East, said, "I moved out of Minneapolis. Here I worked as a female impersonator at the . . ., everybody knew me as. . . . Now nobody knows, back East; I love it."

Disclosure of the Stigma

Since it could be expected that nonpassers disclose their stigma to others on a voluntary basis more frequently than passers, the transsexuals were all asked the following question: *Do you ever voluntarily disclose the fact that until recently you were a biological male and that you have had a conversion operation?*

The answers were surprising. Only two transsexuals, Becky and Elizabeth, admitted to *ever* disclosing their stigma unilaterally. As expected, both were nonpassers. Becky said, "Sometimes I have to. For example to official agencies, like when I applied to my name at City Hall. . . ."

Elizabeth explained, "Only when I have to, like opening a new bank account. . . ."

In addition, it could be expected that passers would want to keep their sex change hidden from more people than nonpassers. For example, some passers may want to prevent disclosure even from their most intimate relationships (husband, children), while nonpassers could be expected to worry mostly about strangers and public disclosure. Therefore the patients were asked the following question: Who are you, or would you be, most reluctant to disclose your recent conversion operation to?

The answers were classified into two categories. On the one hand, a majority of transsexuals said that they would be most reluctant to disclose their sex change to newspapers, strangers and acquaintances. On the other hand there were three individuals who said that they would not even want their husbands, children and good friends to know. As expected, all three transsexuals in this latter category were passers, Sally, Sylvia, and Roberta. Sally was the passing housewife who had not even told her husband. Sylvia was the aspiring housewife who said, "I would never tell my children . . . I'd move as far as possible so they'd never find out!"

Roberta explained: "Oh I suppose a husband probably should know . . . but I wouldn't tell a date!"

Thus most transsexuals did not want to be "fraudulent" with intimate others, but they did wish to avoid public disclosure. In addition, some *passing* transsexuals would go as far as to hide their sex change from sex partners and adoptive children.*

Previous Career

With respect to the transsexuals' previous careers, their postoperative adjustments could be expected to be influenced by at least one factor: transsexuals having had a record of nightclub performances prior to their operation could be expected to become the showbusiness types, while those without such a record could be expected to turn into housewives. Having at first established that all transsexuals had been transvestites except Lee, and that all of them had been homosexuals except Vanessa, it was nevertheless possible to discern different *contexts* in which such behavior had taken place. Some transsexuals had merely been transvestites in the privacy of their homes, for example Monique,

---

*This leaves aside one further possibility. Goffman (1963) has suggested that individuals with a discreditable stigma may prefer to disclose it to distant others rather than to intimate others. Thus, Sally has never told her own husband, but of course the doctors and I, who studied her, know. Similarly Georgette, the alleged transsexual I once gave a ride to (see Chapter 1), decided to confide her deepest secret to me while some of her best friends may not know. In general, people may engage in deeply deviant acts often known to their therapists or to fellow deviants, but not to their parents, marital partners, or children. A prime example of this is given in a recent study of the covert homosexual "tearoom trade" (Humphreys, 1970). It is possible that a covert deviant may wish to protect his most intimate relationships from the potentially devastating effect of disclosure. Only sparse evidence of this was found in the present study. No transsexual plainly indicated that public disclosure would be of little consequence to her as long as her most beloved ones remained ignorant of the truth. The closest approximation of this was provided, as said, by Sally. In addition, Vanessa provides a somewhat similar example. By the time we interviewed her, a growing number of people had learned about her sex change, but she had not (yet?) mustered the courage to tell the truth to her former wife and her family. In fact, she conspired with her daughter to maintain secrecy toward those people.

Elinor, Patricia, and Sylvia. Others, however, had been long-standing professional female impersonators: Linda, Lisa and Maryjo. Also, some e.g. Roberta, had cross-dressed quite overtly yet not commercially, for example as drag queens at homosexual parties.

Since nearly all transsexuals are former transvestites in one form or another, it is not possible to distinguish passers from nonpassers in this respect. However, one thing is clear: if respectability was valued by the patient prior to surgery, it remains important afterwards as well. Thus *overt* transvestites (female impersonators) tend to become stripper types while *covert* transvestites tend to become housewife or aspiring housewife types.

Lisa was the experienced nightclub performer who called herself a former "world-famous female impersonator." As she phrased it, "I was a female impersonator for eighteen years. One of the most famous in America. . . . People still recognize me at the airport. . . ."

Maryjo, too, had worked as a female impersonator for many years. In her own words: "I have been a female impersonator since 1962 . . . I did it all over the United States. . . ."

Renee, finally, had been a majorette in high school. As she explained: "I was state champion baton twirler; I won eighty-three trophies and forty-two medals . . . I taught hundreds of students."

Predictably, Lisa, Maryjo and Renee all became nightclub strippers after their sex changes.

Background

A whole complex of variables that could be expected to influence the way transsexuals adjust as new females was their social background. Many transsexuals were born and raised in the rural Midwest under rigorously puritan conditions. Some moved to the city early, experiencing the liberating influence of cosmopolitan-metropolitan life. Some moved from rural puritanism into the urban underworld. Some merely moved to the city. Some moved to the city only shortly before their operation. Some transsexuals were city-born and city-raised. Some among these have had decades of urban underworld experience, others were middle-class urbanites. Finally, some transsexuals were raised in lower-class families, be they urban or rural, while others came from well-to-do milieus. Thus the transsexuals' postoperative adjustments may be expected to be influenced by their religious, demographic, geographical, occupational and socioeconomic backgrounds.

As far as religous influence is concerned, most transsexuals were not only of such orthodox denominational origins as Lutheranism and Catholicism (see Table I), but many still adhered to their original faith. The minority of transsexuals who claimed not to be influenced by their religious background included Lee, who indicated no religious preference; Rhona, who said "none;" Roberta, who said that it did not matter even though she was originally a Catholic; and Maryjo ("I'm a free believer now"). In addition, Lisa was the only Jew among the group and Linda was the transsexual who had converted to Catholicism for her boyfriend's sake.

With regard to demographic and geographic origins, the majority of transsexuals where born and raised either on the farm or in small towns (see Table I). Those born in large metropolitan centers included Lisa (Chicago), Vanessa (New Orleans) and Patricia, Maryjo and Rhona (Minneapolis). More importantly, some transsexuals had spent most of their lives in their original rural environment, while others had moved to the city many years ago. To the former group belong eight transsexuals. These were not only born in rural areas but also went to high school there, some moving to the city only shortly before their sex conversion. Three transsexuals were born in rural areas but spent most of their lives in the city (having moved there early, or because they are now quite old); these all had college educations.

In terms of socioeconomic status, most transsexuals were of lower-class or lower middle-class origin. Eight transsexuals came from rural lower-class or lower middle-class families. Their fathers were small-town craftsmen, laborers or farmhands. Five respondents came from urban working-class or lower middle-class families. Their fathers were laborers or operatives. Only a few transsexuals came from distinctly upper middle-class families. Their fathers were businessmen or doctors.

While it is difficult to generalize on the basis of the above information, it is possible to discern a certain pattern, as it relates to postoperative adjustment. Typical passers are housewife types and aspiring housewives such as Sally and Sylvia. These transsexuals are all of working-class rural origin, mostly Lutheran. Their educational level is low and their urban experience limited. In brief, they seem to bring with them a baggage of lower middle-class provincialism which may explain part of their efforts at passing and thus achieving what they view as respectability.

On the other hand, typical nonpassers are showbusiness types such as Lisa, and Renee, and career women such as Vanessa. Now these transsexuals tend to be of urban origin, or at least of longlasting urban experience. For example, it is intersting to note that Elizabeth and Sally, two sisters and therefore of similar demographic origin, found themselves on opposite sides of the pass vs. nonpass fence. Elizabeth, a nonpasser and the older one of the two sisters, moved to the city quite a few years back and developed a certain cosmopolitan sophistication as a career woman, which no doubt made her not quite as weary of being an overt transsexual as her sister. On the other hand, Sally, who is a young newcomer to Minneapolis, became a married housewife immediately upon her sex change, and now tries to establish respectability through passing.

Thus we see that urban experience may be associated with nonpassing, i.e. with a lesser amount of preoccupation with respectability. This may, of course, be both psychological and sociological. The urbanite tends to be a nonpasser both because of her own liberated attitudes and because of the urban heterogeneity (Wirth, 1938) which enables her to move freely in many circles.

Corollary to the greater liberalism and sophistication of these transsexuals is the fact that they tend to be better educated, particularly those that follow the career model (*cf.* Vanessa with a Ph.D. and Adelaide with some college), and of higher socioeconomic origin (*cf.* Rhona, a doctor's child and Vanessa, the child of a businessman). Finally, these urban cosmopolites who do not adhere to traditional middle-class standards of respectability with the same rigidity as the passing housewives, are also the ones to take religion relatively lightly.

In sum, the extent to which a transsexual will seek to achieve respectability (through passing, marriage, domestic roles), may be positively related to a protestant, rural, lower middle-class origin, a low level of education and a limited urban experience. On the other hand the urban transsexual tends to be more sophisticated, less provincial and therefore less eager to pass as a natural-born female as a way of achieving respectability. She may be a career woman with a fairly high socioeconomic background and relatively well-educated, or she may be a stripper type with a lower-class urban background and little education. These three possibilities are perhaps best illustrated by Lois, Maryjo and Vanessa:

Lois: Lutheran, born and raised in rural Minnesota, from a lower middle-class family; did not complete high school, went to the city only shortly before her sex conversion. She did cross-dress, but only privately, never as a female impersonator. She is now a passer and an aspiring housewife.*

Maryjo: Born in a metropolitan area from working-class parents; claims no religion, did not complete high school. Not only was she a transvestite, but also a female impersonator for many years around the world. She is now a nonpasser and a stripper.

Vanessa: Born and raised in a large metropolitan area, from a well-to-do business family. She has a Ph.D. Originally a Roman Catholic. Never cross-dressed. She is now a nonpasser, a career woman.

Motives

Probably the first question that comes to mind when dealing with transsexualism is: why? Why do some people decide to change their sex? While psychoanalytic and other types of psychological explanations may offer insights into the etiology of the transsexual's state of mind, there is no consensus about the

---

*In a recent article (Kando, 1972a), I tried to show that transsexuals avoid unbearable conflicts between their social circles of origin, e.g. the family, and their current circles by leading compartmentalized lives. This situation is of course most characteristic of the patients, such as Lois, whose backgrounds are very provincial.

causes of transsexualism. Neither are the etiological differences between homosexuality, transvestism and transsexualism clear. Although Benjamin (1966) and others feel that the various sexual pathologies representing sex and gender role disorientation differ in degree rather than in kind, it is not clear why one individual will choose the life of a covert homosexual,* while another will frequently cross-dress and a third man will desperately seek sex surgery. One thing is agreed upon: the term transsexual refers to individuals who generally think of themselves as members of the sex opposite to that to which they belong biologically at birth; for example, individuals born male but convinced all along that they are female.

In order to engage in a meaningful discussion of the transsexual's motives, "what makes the transsexual tick," it is important to be clear about the concept of motivation (Peters, 1958). Mills (1940) pointed out that *motives,* rather than expressing something which is prior and in the person, can best be viewed as the *terms with which interpretation of conduct by actors proceeds.* Motives are words and they stand for anticipated situational consequences of questioned conduct. In this sense motives are social instruments, i.e. data by modifying which the agent will be able to influence himself and others. They are adequate, consequential and situationally rooted explanations of conduct. Such a conception of motivation is important when examining transsexuals, for these are culturally and psychologically marginal individuals. Questions arise as to what the transsexuals' motives are, and how these motives are altered under their continuing problematic and fluid social conditions.

Considering Mills' conception of motives, and realizing what was said earlier about transsexuals being individuals whose problems are essentially those of *identification,* the best approach to the transsexuals' motives seems to be one that was outlined by Foote (1951). This author notes that while Mills conceives of motives as rationalizations relating conduct to previous experience, this leaves a hiatus open as to how, in fact, language motivates. He agrees with Mills that the basis for motivation is not

---

*For a recent study of covert homosexual behavior, see Humphreys (1970).

drive, tension, energy or need. Nevertheless, in order for behavior to exhibit definiteness and force, which is to say, degree of motivation, there must be some content to the "empty bottle of roles and statuses" enacted by the individual. Now this content, according to Foote, is *identity*. Thus identification, defined as the appropriation of and commitment to a particular identity or series of identities, becomes the basis for motivated conduct.

The establishment of unambiguous identity is the primary source of motivation. This involves naming, the negotiation of problematic aspects of the self and the consensual definition of selves and situations. It involves what other sociologists have called *self-lodging,* i.e. the "lodging of crucial features of one's own identity into structures, into the selves of others and into interaction."* Symbolic interactionism sees each social situation as consisting of the constant moving back and forth of action and objects between (a) self-conscious interpretative action and (b) routinely organized action. It can be expected that routine interaction will be interrupted whenever valued portions of the self are not lodged, recognized and reciprocated. Interaction, then, will consist in large part of renegotiation, relocation and redefinition of selves. Failure at self-lodging may ultimately cause interaction to cease altogether. Such a theoretical perspective on motivation and on the nature of interaction is eminently useful when dealing with transsexuals, whose selves are so highly problematic, and who are continuously engaged in self-conscious self-lodging and identity negotiation.

Since all transsexuals are individuals who say that they have been trapped in the wrong body, they could all be expected to give motives for their sex change which would have to do mostly with their gender identification. At the same time, the different types of transsexuals could be expected to emphasize different motives. To gain information about this, the patients were asked: What were your main reasons for requesting the conversion operation?

The answers revealed indeed the two things that had been anticipated. First, all transsexuals explained their sex change in

---

*A good summary of the symbolic interactionist theory of motivation, incorporating the ideas of Mills and Foote, is provided by Denzin (1969).

terms of the psychiatric and social-psychological vocabulary which defines transsexualism as a state in which the mind is of one sex and the body of the other. Secondly, the different types of transsexuals tended to give somewhat different priorities for having undergone sex surgery.

That the transsexual's primary motive for having undergone sex change is social-psychological and not, for example, sexual is best illustrated by statements such as the following: "I did it for the psychological thing . . . I need the reassurance that I am a woman. I don't have a man to make love to me, and I don't care . . . besides I am kind of scared anyway."

"I wanted to be a woman, whether the sex part was successful or not. I wanted to be of one sex, dress like one, act like one. . . . If I wasn't going with Mike, just knowing that I can function sexually as a woman would be enough."

Furthermore, all transsexuals gave responses indicating that sex change was the inevitable, physiological correction that had to be made, since they were really women all along. Hence, the vast majority of the respondents gave motives such as the following ones: "I'm merely a correction. The words sex change and transsexual are very offensive to me. I can't identify with these terms . . . I don't associate with other transsexuals."

"I've always thought of myself as a female".

"Well, mentally I always thought of myself as a woman. I don't ever remember thinking of myself as a man. . . . I'd always wanted to do it, and the only problem had been financial . . . this didn't cost anything."

Such motives, then, were given by all transsexuals, regardless of the type to which they belong. The establishment of a harmonious gender identification and self-concept was of utmost importance to all of them, and the sex change as well as its postoperative interpretation were the major stratagems in establishing the desired identification. This, much more than alternative motives such as sexual gratification, monetary rewards or social success, was essentially the rationale given by the transsexuals for having changed sex.

However, transsexuals did place somewhat different emphases on various motives, depending on their type. Benjamin (1966) already found that young transsexuals are more likely to seek sex change as a result of *sexual* considerations, older transsexuals are motivated by their gender distortion, i.e. by *psychological* reasons. The *legal* motive is present in all transsexuals, but most of all among transvestites since they risk prosecution for their habit, and the *social* motive, finally, is predominant among those who, as men, are embarrassed by their conspicuous feminine physique and appearance.

Following a somewhat similar line of thought I attempted to establish differences between the motives given by the various types of transsexuals distinguished in this study. As indicated earlier, all transsexuals gave social-psychological and psychiatric motives that explained their behavior in terms of identification and self-concept. However, one significant deviation occurred: three transsexuals, Maryjo, Becky, and Rhona, emphasized the purely *sexual.* Maryjo was a good-looking twenty-nine-year-old single brunette working as a stripper, of working-class metro-politan origin. Becky was a twenty-three year old cocktail waitress, also of urban background. Rhona, finally, was another twenty-nine year old stripper of long-standing urban experience. Thus significantly, all three transsexuals giving straightforward sexual motives for their sex change were nonpassers, younger than the sample average, urban sophisticates, and working in nightclubs.

Methods of Information Management

We have compared passers and nonpassers along a number of variables. The question at this point is: how does the *passing* transsexual manage information about herself? In this section we shall examine a number of devices used by the transsexual when she passes, and therefore must manage information about herself.

Although the extent to which transsexuals pass varies from cases in which they may be known to be transsexuals by all their acquaintances, to cases in which not even the most intimate relations knows, every transsexual experiences situations in which others have no reason to assume that she is anything but a female. If nowhere else, this will occur at least as she commutes to work, walks down the street, or participates in other mass, anonymous behavior requiring no self-identification beyond the exhibition of standard physical identity attributes. Furthermore, it has already been shown that transsexuals tend to pass as natural-born females increasingly as time goes on.

Some of the processes involved in passing are one-shot events. The passer undergoes a ritual, changes names, titles, jobs, moves to a new community, acquires a new circle of friends, etc. These and other similar moves are single, decisive steps that make a more or less permanent contribution to the passer's new statuses and identity. In other respects, however, passing constitutes an ongoing and perhaps never-ending effort. The continued maintenance of a certain amount of social distance, the continued vigilant screening of one's statements, the constant use of distortions, euphemisms, little lies (Garfinkel, 1967) and the redefinition of past events for the construction of a *currently* acceptable biography, all these are methods which transsexuals and other passers employ as they continue to achieve and maintain their new status(es). Thus it can be said of the transsexual at any time that she has passed and that she is passing.

As far as the first facet of passing is concerned — the one-time passage from male to female status — this involves at least the following four historical events: a distinct and ritualized status passage; the temporary coaching of the passer by experts, professionals or other significant others; geographical mobility; and job mobility. The second facet of passing — the continuing achievement of female status and identity — consists of a vast number of skills in which transsexuals will presumably excel as time goes by, skills that involve mostly the management of information about oneself. These methods include the maintenance of social distance, various forms of lying, the use of accomplices, the use of euphemisms, the substitution of lesser stigmas for the real thing, dissociation from the in-group and from other contaminating groups, and biographical reconstruction.

Status Passage

The most evident manifestation of the transsexual's passage from male to female is her assumption of a new name. The fact that her status passage involves the assumption not of new titles but of new names, which are then duly legally recorded, sets it in one category with marriage. The fact that, unlike marriage, it is irreversible, places her status passage in one category with death.

While it is practical requirement that urges the transsexual to assume a new, feminine, name, the type of first name(s) she chooses indicates some of the ritualism involved in there status passage. In order to discover what this name change means to the transsexuals, they were asked their former given names, their new names, and their reasons for the choice of their new names.

The findings indicate that in some cases the new name is merely the feminized version of the old name; in other cases it is as new a name as possible so as to establish the greatest possible distance between old and new identity. In other cases yet, the new name symbolizes some personal attachment. In no case is the new name chosen randomly. In Table X, I have tried to give a pseudonymous approximation of the interviewed transsexuals' old and new Christian names. The table allows us to gauge the continuity in the

Table X

TRANSSEXUALS' CHRISTIAN NAMES, BEFORE AND AFTER
CONVERSION OPERATION (PSEUDONYMS)

Before	After
Michael	Monique
Eldon	Elinor
Patrick	Patricia
Adolf	Adelaide
Ed	Elizabeth
Larry	Linda
Leroy	Lisa
John	Jane
Louis	Lois
	Maryjo
Richard	Sylvia
Bob	Roberta
Jim	Lee
Van	Vanessa
Kevin	Becky
John	Joan
Michael	Rhona

transsexuals' identity as expressed in their name change.

Clearly, several of the patients simply chose the feminized version of their original given name (Patrick became Patricia, John became Jane, *etc.*). However, some indicated that they had chosen a certain name precisely because it did not evoke any past association. Adelaide, for example, said that she chose that name because she did not know anybody who had it.

Sylvia's comments about her name change indicate similar feelings: "I used to be called. . . . My father named me after a baseball player in Oregon. He wanted me to be a baseball player, I guess [laughs hilariously]. Now my name is Sylvia. I always liked that name . . . it's pretty and feminine, not like. . . ."

The wish to pass may be a reason for *not* choosing a feminized version of one's former name. For example Rhona used to be Michael and she performed as a female impersonator under the name Michele. She wrote to us, explaining: "I dropped Michele, my former stage name, because it was too well-known. . . ."

Those who did opt for a feminized version of their former boy's name were often unaware of that fact. For example, Patricia, who used to be Patrick, said: "This is just my mother's middle name . . . I wasn't aware of the coincidence that the names are similar."

Linda, who used to be Larry, explained her name change as follows: "My family decided on my new names. . . . I don't particularly care for my first name. . . ."

Jane, who used to be John, said: "Why Jane for a new name? It starts with the same initial."

Indeed, the preservation of the former initials was a convenience that determined many transsexuals' new name choices. As Lisa explained: "My new name? One day the nurse just took down my old name and put up Lisa. It has the same initial so I just kept it."

Sex conversion, as other drastic status passage, is conceived as a rebirth. Consequently many transsexuals feel and act young even though their real age ranges from twenty-one to well over fifty. They do not seem to be aware of their chronological age and view the sex conversion not only as passage from male to female, but also a return to youth. One attractive brunette whose twenty-nine years indeed do not show, said: "I feel that I am only one year old . . . I feel I was reborn. . . . I don't feel my age and that's good because I feel I've been cheated out of so much in life. . . ."

Sylvia expresses her euphoria differently: "I'm very thrilled about it [the conversion]. It seems like a dream come true."

Another transsexual added: "All of a sudden I'm young again, I want tomorrow, I want some more time."

Coaching

Transsexuals were asked to mention the individuals who had been most important, influential and/or helpful in connection with the sex conversion and in connection with learning how to become women. To summarize the findings the answers were coded into the following categories:

1. Professional Coaches: Priests, counselors, psychologists, psychiatrists, M.D.'s, surgeons, *etc.* All people who had somehow played a professional role in the transsexual's status passage, not only in connection with her sex conversion but also at much earlier stages of her identity crisis. All individuals mentioned in this category happened to be male.

2. Women: Female friends and relatives, including mother and sisters.

3. Male Sex Partners: Boyfriend or husband.

4. Other Male Friends

5. Other Transsexuals and Transvestites

The frequencies of the various responses were as follows:
1. Ten transsexuals mentioned thirteen professional coaches.
2. Nine transsexuals mentioned ten women.
3. Five transsexuals mentioned five male sex partners.
4. Four transsexuals mentioned seven other male friends.
5. Three transsexuals mentioned five other transsexuals or transvestites.

Altogether, fourteen transsexuals mentioned forty individuals.

The tabulation indicates that the most frequent role in the transsexual's status passage has been played by professional "coaches." The most frequent reference by far was to Dr. Donald Hastings, head psychiatrist at the University of Minnesota in charge of the project, but other medics were also mentioned. In general, doctors, psychiatrists and even surgeons were seen not only in their professional functions, but also as teachers. That every one of these "coaches" mentioned was a male is probably due to the nature of the occupational distribution in our society. Within their own families, however, transsexuals have received more inspiration from females than from males, as was to be expected. A majority mentioned female relatives as having played an important and sympathetic role in their status passage, but *none* mentioned male relatives. A typical response was given by Patricia, who said: "My husband has been very important (in helping me to prepare for my new life as a woman) . . . I lived with him for four years before the operation. . . . Also my mother, and Dr. Hastings."

As in most other instances, Patricia's main source of inspiration and help in her gender passage had been a female relative (her mother), her sex partner and the psychiatrist. These, then, are the most typical significant others mentioned by transsexuals in connection with their social-psychological feminization.

What the above tabulation does not reflect is the fact that many transsexuals felt that they had mostly gone it alone. Monique, for instance, said that she had had to rely on herself entirely, not even receiving moral support or coaching from her mother. Maryjo was even more emphatic: "People who coached me? Are you kidding? Who would have to coach me to want to do something I've wanted all my life! I was the only person important to myself. . . . I hope I'm not a self-centered person but the help I got was mostly from myself. . . ."

Geographical Mobility

A simple test showed that transsexuals are more mobile than nontranssexuals. Since status passage and stigma concealment so frequently involve moving far away from one's location of origin, this could indeed be expected to apply to transsexuals. The entire sample of males, females and transsexuals was asked whether they had moved to a different city or state within the past year. The findings and the test of significance are reproduced in Table XI.

Table XI

"HAVE YOU MOVED TO A DIFFERENT CITY OR STATE WITHIN THE PAST YEAR?"

	Yes	No	Total
Normals	4	30	34
Transsexuals	7	10	17
Total	11	40	51

Chi Square = 4.21 (corrected for continuity)

df   = 1

P   <   .02 (one-tailed)

Table XI indicates that transsexuals are significantly more mobile than normals. It might be argued that transsexuals are a particularly mobile (unstable?) population and that *this* produced the data in Table XI rather than their status passage. The facts indicate otherwise. In the first place, most transsexuals had undergone sex surgery during the past year, so that their high degree of mobility during that same period must be viewed as related to their sex conversion. Moreover, many patients clearly indicated that they had moved, or intended to move, *after* their conversion operation precisely in order to facilitate status passage. While several transsexuals moved into the Twin Cities shortly before their operations and can now therefore pass as natural females without much threat of disclosure in that metropolitan area, a majority of them moved *after* the operation as well. This is the case of all five respondents who could only be interviewed by mail. It is also the case of those who had not yet left at the time of the interview, but were planning to do so, and whose imminent mobility is not reflected in Table XI. As one transsexual said: "I hope to get out soon . . . like I don't want to advertise myself. I run into too many people . . . I'm only waiting for my birth certificate to be changed."

Occupational Mobility

That sex change generally means job change seems inescapable. Among the eleven transsexuals who were employed at the time of our interviews, only Vanessa had retained her former job. However, even this was not without difficulty and some prejudicial treatment, as the reader may recall (see Chapter 3).

All other transsexuals thought it inevitably necessary to change jobs in connection with their sex change. Sylvia, for example, when asked why she changed jobs after the sex conversion, said: "Mostly because I just couldn't . . . I didn't exactly know how to tell my former boss. . . ."

Another transsexual, a hairdresser, had a boss who she said, ". . . hated the idea of me being a transsexual so much that I had to change jobs. . . . I took up a new job only half a block away from where I had been working before, but I had to get a new job!"

There is, of course a considerable amount of occupational *continuity* in most transsexuals' pre- and postoperative lives. Most transsexuals had difficulty playing male roles prior to their sex change. This, after all, is the essence of their pathology. Understandably, many already held less than fully masculine occupations — hairdressers, beauticians, dancers, *etc.;* for these individuals occupational continuity was not difficult to accomplish. Only those transsexuals who had distinctly masculine occupational roles prior to their conversion (for example, Roberta, the business executive), may have encountered the extra problem of having to learn a new trade that is more appropriate to their new gender. Most typical of the job continuity of transsexuals are the female impersonators and overt transvestites who become strippers. Renee, for example, said, "Previous to surgery I lived as a female [transvestite] for seven years. I had two successful businesses that I owned and operated as a woman. . . . Now I am a dancer and baton twirler downtown. . . ."

While the stripper thus highlights occupational continuity in the transsexual's life, at the same time she represents passing behavior. Only two transsexuals (Renee and Helen) advertised themselves as transsexuals in their nightclubs. More typical was Lisa, the huge fifty-year-old transsexual who had been a female impersonator prior to her operation, who now had a singing act in an Eastern nightclub and who said: "I love all the people in Winnipeg . . . but they don't know. I think it's disgusting to advertise yourself as a sex change, like Renee. . . ."

Maryjo, who had also been a female impersonator prior to her sex change, now worked as a stripper in a local nightclub. Like Lisa, she opted against the commercial exploitation of the sex change itself: ". . . I have to pretend, when I am on stage . . . I'm a stripper."

Thus continuing work in the same general line, as do the strippers, does not mean that status passage is not taking place. In fact, it is possible that a gradual cycle of passing might be taking place, whereby transsexuals go though a succession of positions, beginning with one that is fairly close to their former status and ending, gradually, in positions of respectable womanhood that entail total status passage. Sylvia, for example, had already had two jobs since her sex change. As she explained: "I stayed at the place [first job] for six months . . . then they found out. . . . It was a company that dealt with homosexual merchandise. . . . Then I changed to this one [Sylvia is now secretary to a nun] . . . on my new job nobody knows. . . ."

A ritualized status change, a period of coaching, geographical mobility and occupational mobility are events that accompany the transsexual's status passage at and around the time of her sex conversion. In addition, a number of passing devices may be expected to continue to operate into the foreseeable future, as methods used by the transsexual to safeguard her new identity. These techniques may include social distance, lying, enlisting accomplices, using euphemisms, stigma substitution, dissociating oneself from the "own" and various biographical reconstructions.

Social Distance

A comparison of males, females and transsexuals revealed that the latter tend to have fewer "really good friends" than normals. This could, of course, mean that transsexuals are truly alienated individuals, or that they at least feel that way. While such may

very well be the case, some of the patients' answers do indicate
that the lack of social intimacy in their lives sometimes has to do
with stigma concealment. Sylvia, for example, said, "Some of the
closest friends are at work . . . a couple of other secretaries. . . ."
But these secretaries do not know.

Similarly, Lisa's numerous "real good friends" are all conveniently distant. In her own words: "I have about twenty real
good friends . . . they're scattered all over the United States. . . ."
Presumably these distant friends do not know.

Renee's case is similar. "Right now," she explains, "I'm living in
an apartment building with nothing but girls. Only my roommate
knows. . . . With my other friends it's all girl talk. . . ."

Thus, whether the transsexual has many "really good friends"
or not (and she generally does not), such friendship does not cover
full identity disclosure.

Lying

Unlike the act of omission involved in the above cases, lying is
an act of *comission.* Here the transsexual does not only avoid
disclosing her sex change, but she in fact denies it and invents
events to explain anomalies. This is done for example by the
strippers and prostitutes who claim natural femininity. It is also
illustrated by Sally, who married shortly after her conversion
operation under the guise of being a natural female. She still has
not told her husband. She does not worry about the possible
(legal) consequences of the misrepresentation; thus far she has
come up with the right answers at the right time when questioned
by her husband. For example she told him that her inability to
bear children is due to a recent hysterectomy. Since he also knew
of her recent hospitalization, she told him that it had been
precisely for that purpose. Thus, the two lies conveniently
supported one another.

Vanessa has also found it necessary to lie, but, unlike Sally, she
lied not to her present marital partner but to her former partner,
i.e. to the former wife. Vanessa's sex change was the culmination
of long-range planning. She had been married twenty-five years,
had a nineteen-year-old daughter, obtained a divorce in 1968 and

was hospitalized shortly thereafter. However, the wife was never told the true reason for requesting the divorce and the true cause for hospitalization. At the time of the interview, the former wife was still under the belief that the divorce was the result of incompatibility and that Vanessa — still known to her as John — had been hospitalized for some illness. In Vanessa's own words: "Rose, my wife, doesn't know yet . . . she knew of cross-dressing, but she was content with the marriage, as bad as it was for me. . . . I still talk to her and we still have the common interest of the daughter . . . but I did go into the hospital under some pretext. . . ."

Accomplices

Again Vanessa provides a good example of this. Not only has she lied to her former wife about the reasons for requesting a divorce and the nature of the surgery, but she also deliberately asked her daughter to help her in that endeavor. Paula, the daughter, had found out that her father had undergone sex change. In Vanessa's own words: ". . . as far as Paula is concerned, what brought it to a head is, she called me one time and asked me, 'Are we going to get together, because remember, 15th is Father's Day.' And I said 'Paula, of course I love you very much, but I do have to tell you that I can no longer accept Father's Day gifts. . . .' So I explained the whole story, we had a very long conversation about it. . . . I asked her to, at least for the present, maintain secrecy just between us, until the appropriate time to advise Rose that surgery took place."

Vanessa used the complicity of her daughter to hide her sex change from those who still knew her as a man. The opposite procedure is more frequent: transsexuals often use others to pass as women. The psychiatrist — who knows — may be asked to state that the transsexual is a bona fide female; a husband, who knows, may have to explain to the transsexual's in-laws that they deliberately decided not to have children; an employer who knows may introduce the transsexual to her job peers as a lady who has just recovered from a serious illness, or who just moved to town. In each case, the transsexual's passage to female status benefits from the lies of these accomplices.

Euphemisms

The use of euphemisms and rationalizations is sometimes necessitated by the transsexual's self-concept. For example, a majority of them reject the terms "conversion operation," "sex change" and "transsexualism," and label their operation *corrective surgery*. Unlike the other terms, this label implies that the surgery has merely rectified a minor physiological aberration, a correction needed to achieve something which nature had intended in the first place, but which they had been deprived of through an unfortunate accident. Thus by rejecting the primacy of biology over psychology, transsexuals claim natural femininity and give to their "corrective surgery" the same type of legitimacy as the surgical removal of any other physical defect. One result is the ability to think of oneself as a true female. As Elizabeth puts it: "The term transsexual doesn't offend me, but I'm of one sex so it's inapproriate."

Other euphemisms include the reduction of various forms of conflict to "problems of communication" and the denial of the importance of sexual intercourse. Thus a transsexual may argue that she had to change jobs because of "communication problems" rather than as a result of having become unacceptable to colleagues who knew her as a male. Or, if unable to have sexual intercourse without giving herself away (some of the artificial vaginas are not properly formed), she may abstain and claim that the psychological rewards of being a full-fledged woman are more important anyway. This means playing up the psychological components of gender identity and playing down the physical ones. In each of the above cases, the transsexual rationalizes away or minimizes, through euphemisms, the importance of some event in such a manner that she may continue to feel that (a) she is a woman, that (b) others should accept her as a woman, and that (c) she basically shares normally and sufficiently in the female experience.

Stigma Substitution

A further method in the transsexual's self-presentation is the substitution of lesser stigmas for the real thing. Goffman has suggested that stigmatized individuals may present their stigma signs as signs of some other, less serious stigma. As far as transsexuals are concerned, this means that some subjects may opt for roles that are deviant, but less deviant than that of being a transsexual. Many of the patients possessed such stigmatizing roles as stripper, former mental patient or felon's wife. These stigmas came, of course, in addition to the already burdensome trans-sexual identity. However, in some cases they provided an opportunity for stigma substitution. Maryjo, for example, said, "Right now I am living in an apartment building, with nothing but girls. Only my roommate knows. With my other friends it's all girl talk; but there is a problem, you know how society looks down on strippers!"

What is so significant in Maryjo's statement is that her self-concept is that of the socially stigmatized, and therefore ostracized, but as a stripper, which is less serious than as a transsexual!

The continued affiliation of many transsexuals with various blemishing subcultures may represent movement from a category of extreme deviance into a class of lesser deviance. The new stigma, while representing a certain continuity in the transsexual's life and overall alienation from middle-class society, is nevertheless seen as less burdensome than the initial one. Being a convict's wife, a junkie's mistress or a prostitute are somewhat more frequent, more familiar and less extravagant stigmas than being a sex change.

Dissociation From the "Own"

Transsexuals may further protect their new identity by dis-sociating themselves from one another and from any other contaminating group. The "own" are generally other members of the transsexual-transvestite subculture that centers around a number of downtown stripjoints and gay bars. It is from this in-group that many transsexuals wish to remove themselves. Some simply prefer not to frequent other transsexuals. Some typical quotes: "As far as other transsexuals are concerned, we hinder each other, we don't do each other any good. We don't behave well en masse."

"I know most other transsexuals. I met most of them here [at the hospital] . . . I have been back here for surgery six times. But socially I don't see them too often. We chat once in a while, they're friends. You know, birds of a feather flock together, but we don't always get along. Most of them move around quite a bit. . . . Most transsexuals love only themselves. My sister and I are different."

"Yes, I feel that I am better than the other ones. I have better morals . . . most transsexuals here in Minneapolis are pigs. They have no moral standards."

"I don't socialize with other transsexuals . . . they tend to be cliquish. . . ."

Transsexuals not only dissociate themselves from other transsexuals as they work to establish female identity, but they are equally reluctant to be identified with other sexually deviant categories — homosexuals, transvestites — since such identification is potentially contaminating. Examples of such statements: "As a teen-ager in high school, I began homosexual acts, but not with homos; with normal guys, with friends . . . I hate homosexuals, I never wanted sex with them. They are pigs. I no longer tolerate them. Homos get what they deserve!"

"I cross-dressed ever since I was sixteen. But I wasn't a transvestite either; it didn't do anything for me sexually. . . ."

Thus, even though transsexuals may *de facto* have been homosexuals and transvestites, they tend to reinterpret those acts as natural, heterosexual, female behavior. This enables them postoperatively to dissociate themselves from homosexuals and transvestites.

Biographical Reconstruction and the Definition of the Situation

The reinterpretation of earlier homosexual or transvestite acts as actually being the normal, heterosexual acts of a woman also highlights the final method discussed in the present chapter: the transsexual's biographical redefinitions which will satisfactorily account for who she presently is.

The object of the transsexual's biographical reconstructions is twofold: On the one hand, she must come up with a life history that will be more or less acceptable as that of a normal female. On the other hand she must account for having become a transsexual. The two objectives are contradictory, but no more contradictory than the transsexual's identity itself. Since she wishes to be identified as a normal (female) but realizes that she is a deviant (transsexual), she is involved in biographical reconstructions that support her present identity both as a normal and as a deviant. On the one hand she defines autobiographical events in such a way that they support her contention that she has always been a woman, and on the other hand she also formulates facts and events which explain "what went wrong," i.e. why she became a transsexual. The latter task is accomplished mostly with the help of psychiatrists and psychoanalytic rhetoric.

The first category of biographical reconstructions, then, consists of demonstrations that one has always been a woman. For example, Sally said: "Even before the operation I've always identified as a woman. I went dressed as a woman, used women's bathrooms. . . ."

Lisa felt the same way: "I found that I was a beautiful woman trapped in a fat man's body. . . ."

Consequently, what to us may seem to have been homosexual acts was, in the transsexual's mind, normal female heterosexual behavior. As Renee expressed it: "Previous to surgery I lived as a female. . . . I dated men only, but I was never a homosexual in any form. I went to gay bars twice in my entire life. I was not accepted by gay society, nor did I wish to be . . . I was a woman."

More complex is the array of biographical reconstructions that serve to explain "what went wrong," i.e. why she became a transsexual. Here, the transsexual, with the aid of a vulgarized Freudianism picked up in various psychiatrists' offices, endeavors to create a plausible etiology for her final condition of transsexualism. Since it is an etiology that is being constructed, this implies that the transsexual views transsexualism as a pathology. Thus while on the one hand she argues that she has been a female all along, on the other hand she is deeply convinced that she is a deviant.

This double bind is not apparent to her. Her claim to natural womanhood is in the face of blatent biographical contradictions. Renee, for example, was born in rural Minnesota. In high school she became a champion baton twirler. She went on to beauty college and began, only then, to cross-dress. She has lived as a female since then, cohabitating with a boyfriend during the past three years. On the basis of this biography, Renee claimed that she was always a female. But then, she felt the need to explain that her parents raised her in an effeminate fashion, that her mother had always been domineering and that she never had a close male identity figure.

The repeated use of such "sad tale" accounts* reveals that transsexuals in fact consider themselves the victims of faulty socialization, and not the healthy females who need nothing but minor corrective surgery. In this process, all respondents blamed others for what had happened to them. The mother was by far the most frequent target. Others considered responsible included the father, other relatives and friends. Sally, for example, explained her relationship to her mother as follows: "I was never close to my mother . . . she has always been proud of having given birth to a first born son (my brother). . . . She always wore the pants in the family. When she was carrying me, she had only girls' names picked (so she must have wanted a girl). . . . She was never happy as a woman. . . ."

Roberta felt the same way: "I rather think that my mother wanted a girl when I was born. . . ."

Thus the mother is held accountable for some of the things that went wrong. At the same time, the relationship to the father has also allegedly been problematic. As Sally explained: "My father worked nights and slept during the day. I never saw much of him . . . I was mother's pet."

Lois also blamed her father for the unfortunate turn of events: "[he] insisted that I should marry my stepmother's niece and settle down. We only lived together for about one year. During that time we were separated four or five times. I dated guys all along, before and during my marriage. When I got married my attitude was: 'I'll show them (my parents) it's not gonna

---

*For a typology of accounts, including the "sad tale" see Lyman and Scott (1970).

work. . . .' We didn't have sex. . . ."

Sylvia makes other serious accusations: "I was in a mental hospital for three years. My father had me committed when I was eighteen. He wouldn't let me out till the doctors put the pressure on him."

In some cases, someone outside the family is held responsible for certain developments. Vanessa said: "I'd been going with Rose during college years as a date. And I'd been living with Fritz. I had met Fritz prevous to the age of twenty-one and it was under his influence that I went to college and then after that he sort of urged me that I wouldn't get ahead as a young man unless I was married and I had been dating Rose, so it was kind of expected that we'd be married, and we were."

Some transsexuals' self-analyses and etiologies are more sophisticated. Vanessa, for example, explained: "I was being schizophrenic, like in *Three Faces of Eve*. I didn't know who I was in the morning, when I got up, whether I was John or Vanessa. . . . Now there is no John left, only a sense of relief. In other words I suffered from schizophrenia. . . . John is somebody that's gone away now, that I remember very nicely. . . ."

Finally, there are various other biographical exaggerations that contribute to an overall "sad tale." Lisa, for example, claimed to have been married under the following conditions: "I was married to a woman before the operation, but marriage was never consummated. I was married three times, at sixteen, at eighteen and at thirty-eight. I never consummated any of them. I wanted to be something else. My wives were rich, they supported me. Then they got tired of waiting and got divorces. . . . My first marriage lasted only a month, the second only three months, the third one a year."

In sum, most transsexuals seem to have reconstructed their biographies in such a manner that their becoming transsexuals is understandable. Many have worked out an etiology for their gender condition, often borrowing vulgarized psychoanalytic motives that stress faulty childhood socialization, particularly the alleged unresolved Oedipal relationship. The mother may then alternatively be described as rejecting or overly protective, as either too feminine or too masculine. The main point is that she is

given an important role in the sad series of events that lead to
transsexualism. These etiological accounts explaining the
pathology are given, while at the same time transsexuals claim that
there is nothing wrong with them, that they have been females all
along and that sex surgery was merely "corrective."

In addition, some of the subjects felt that the tensions they now
had to endure were simply those of every normal female. For
example, the shyness and inevitable prudishness many of them
now felt were supposed to be, after all, appropriate feminine
characteristics. As Lois put it, when discussing intimate contact
with other women: ". . . I wouldn't undress in front of a woman, I
wouldn't strip with anyone else around, but I think most women
would feel this way toward each other."

Finally, tension was sometimes simply denied. Some transsexuals maintained that: ". . . those people that we've told, it
doesn't make any difference to them."

Summary and Conclusion

All transsexuals bear stigma that is sometimes known, but
sometimes hidden. They all pass at times, but are known as
transsexuals at other times. Which strategy is considered more
feasible and more advantageous depends on the situation and on
the individual. Some choose to pass as natural-born females in as
many situations as possible, doing this with increasing frequency
as time goes on. Others see greater advantages in exhibiting and
exploiting their sex change, most notably the strippers.

In this chapter I have tried to establish some differences
between transsexuals who often attempt to pass and those who do
not. How do we account for the fact that Sally is a housewife
whose husband does not know, while Renee works as a stripper
and part-time prostitute, advertising her sex change in public?
Surely it is no coincidence that most housewives and aspiring
housewife types are among the passers, while most nonpassers are
strippers. There are, then, essentially two possibilities open to the
feminized transsexual: to pass or not to pass. It is now possible to
sketch a brief composite picture of the typical passer and the
typical nonpasser.

The passer has generally undergone sex change earlier than the nonpasser. Her surgery went smoothly and was highly successful so that she is now an attractive and feminine female who does not run much risk of "being read" and who is, in fact, seldom taken for a man, although this may occur over the telephone. She is generally young and she has moved recently and far away from her place of origin. She rarely discloses her stigma of her own volition, but if she does, it is to someone she knows well, for example to a fiance. She has cross-dressed in the past, but only as a covert transvestite, not as a nightclub female impersonator. She is likely to be of rural, working-class or lower middle-class origin, brought up in and still adhering to some orthodox faith, and with not much formal education. She brings with her a set of provincial attitudes and a rigid conception of respectability. She explains her sex conversion as something that had to be done in order for her to achieve the harmonious female identity which she was entitled to all along.

On the other hand, the typical nonpassing transsexual has undergone sex surgery recently. Because of possible surgical difficulties, or perhaps because she had a robust and masculine physique to begin with, or also maybe because she was generally fairly old at the time of her sex change, this transsexual's physical femininity leaves something to be desired. She is therefore more often mistaken for a male. Conceiving of her sex change less as a total rebirth, she may not have moved after her operation, at least not far away. She may openly admit that she is a sex change, even to the public, as in the stripper's case. She engages in a nightclub career because she is likely to have been employed as a female impersonator before her operation. She is likely to be of urban origin, or at least of long-lasting urban experience. She may be of upper or lower socioeconomic origin and she may be poorly or well-educated. At any rate her values are those of the urban sophisticate, which means that strict religous adherence is not in her line, that she is not terribly persistent in trying to establish middle-class respectability, and that she is sometimes comfortable with a vocabulary of motives that explains her sex change in plain sexual terms.

Finally, when it came to passing as a natural-born female and managing information about one's gender identity, two types of phenomena were found to have occured among transsexuals. On the one hand they have taken a number of specific, one-time steps to achieve female status; on the other hand, they can be expected to *continue* to protect their newly acquired gender identity through the use of a variety of ongoing social methods.

The first category of passing steps includes name change; conceiving of the status passage as a rebirth; a period of coaching by professionals, friends or relatives; geographical mobility; and job change.

The second category of passing devices consists of more or less recurring processes that transsexuals engage in. These include the maintenance of social distance (having few intimate friends), lying, the use of accomplices, the use of euphemisms or rationalizations, the substitution of lesser stigmas for the real ones, dissociation from the in-group as well as from other contaminating groups such as homosexuals and transvestites, biographical reconstructions to account for the pathology, as well as biographical reconstructions that will prove that one has always been a female.

Also, transsexuals have a tendency to define their situation as rosily as possible. Most concur that things are now much easier than prior to surgery (which may be true), and some deny that there is tension when interacting with others (which is not true).*

REFERENCES

Becker, Howard and Strauss, Anselm L.: Careers, personality and adult socialization. Am J Sociol, November:253-263, 1956.

Benjamin, Harry: The Transsexual Phenomenon. New York, The Julian Press, 1966.

Denzin, Norman K.: Symbolic interactionism and ethnomethodology: A proposed synthesis. Am Sociol Rev, Dec.:922-934, 1969.

Foote, Nelson N.: Identification as the basis for a theory of motivation. Am Sociol Rev, February:14-21, 1951.

Goffman, Erving: Stigma: Notes on the Management of Spoiled Identity. Englewood Cliffs, N.J., Prentice Hall, 1963.

Griffin, John Howard: Black Like Me. Boston, Houghton Mifflin, 1960.

Humphreys, Laud: Tearoom Trade. Chicago, Aldine, 1970.

---

*For a study that deals with levels of tolerance and intolerance toward various aspects of transsexualism, and with responses to such attitudes, see Kando (1972b).

Kando, Thomas: Passing and stigma management: The case of the transsexual. Sociol Q, Fall:475-483, 1972a.

——— The projection of intolerance: A comparison of males, females and transsexuals. Journal of Sex Research, August:225-236, 1972b.

Linton, Ralph: The Study of Man: An Introduction. New York, Appleton-Century-Crofts, 1936.

Lyman, Stanford M., and Scott, Marvin B.: A Sociology of the Absurd. New York, Appleton-Century-Crofts, 1970.

Mills, C. Wright: Situated actions and vocabularies of motive. Am Sociol Rev, December:904-913, 1940.

Myrdal, Gunnar: An American Dilemma. New York, Harper and Row, 1962.

Peters, R. S.: The Concept of Motivation. London, Routledge and Kegan Paul, 1958.

Strauss, Anselm L.: Mirrors and Masks. Glencoe, Ill., The Free Press, 1959.

Wirth, Louis: Urbanism as a way of life. Am J Sociol, July:1-24, 1938.

Chapter 5

STIGMA AND
TENSION MANAGEMENT

To the fundamental sociological characteristics of the transsexual experience belong stigma and passing. Unless absolutely no one knows that the transsexual is a transsexual, she belongs to a stigmatized minority. However, she has *de facto* been converted from male to female and she sometimes tries to truly pass, i.e. conceal her former gender identity. Thus, on some occasions the transsexual bears a known stigma and in other cases she conceals it.

Goffman (1963) defines stigma as an attribute that is deeply discrediting and incongruous with our stereotype of what a given type of individual should be. He suggests several social mechanisms that may operate when stigma is present. Furthermore he distinguishes between two types of stigma, or two types of stigmatized individuals — the discredited and the discreditable. The first case occurs when the stigmatized individual assumes his differentness is known about already or evident on the spot; the second possibility is when the individual assumes his stigma is neither known to those present nor immediately perceivable by them.

Goffman's distinction between the discreditable and the discredited seems to parallel our distinction between the passer and the nonpasser, or at least between a situation in which passing occurs, or is attempted or contemplated, and one where it is not.

This raises the second fundamental feature of the transsexual's experience: passing. It is clear that these individuals straddle Goffman's distinction. In some situations they engage in passing — then being merely discreditable — while in other situations they do not — resigning themselves to being discredited. Goffman suggests

118

that the discredited — not attempting to pass — must find ways to manage tension, while the discreditable — engaged in passing — must manage information. Realizing that the same transsexual is likely to be engaged in both the management of known stigma and the achievement of status passage at different times, we must examine the responses of all transsexuals in an effort to see how each manages both tension and information.

The Self-imposition of Stigma

Goffman describes three different types of stigma: abominations of the body, blemishes of individual character inferred from a known record, and tribal stigmas such as race and ethnicity. The transsexual's stigma does not fit any one of these types. All we may say is that it straddles the boundary between physical and characterological stigmas. This is to say that any tension in interaction resulting from the transsexual's stigma must be caused either by noticeable physical deformities or by the sheer knowledge others have of the transsexual.

The physical nature of the transsexual's stigma was dealt with earlier in the study. Some among them are good-looking and feminine, and they should not have any trouble passing as natural-born females. Others, however, remain odd in manners and appearance. A simple statistical comparison of transsexuals and normals established beyond doubt that the physical appearance of transsexuals indeed remains more problematic than that of normals. Respondents were asked the following question: *Have you, in the past year, been mistaken for a member of the opposite sex? How often?* Table XII shows the result of this test.

While a significant portion of the transsexuals appears to have problematic physiques, we should note that a majority of them do not. Most transsexuals are definitely feminine in attire, appearance and manners. They may generally be large and in some cases unnaturally heavily made up in order to conceal facial hair, but there can be no doubt in most cases that they are, indeed, women. Several were sufficiently feminine to be strippers and among these, Maryjo, Linda and Rhona did not advertise themselves as transsexuals. Sally, of course, was married to a man who is not

Table XII

"HAVE YOU, IN THE PAST YEAR, BEEN MISTAKEN FOR A MEMBER
OF THE OPPOSITE SEX? HOW OFTEN?"

	Normals	*Transsexuals*	*Total*
Never	33	10	43
Once or More	1	7	8

Chi Square = 9.83 (corrected for continuity)
df   = 1
P   <   .01

aware of her sex change. Bobbie, Cleo and perhaps others were able to operate as prostitutes incognito. Apparently many transsexuals have become sufficiently feminine physically to pass the test of the sex act itself. Thus, in many cases the transsexual's stigma is social-psychological rather than physical. It is only our *knowledge* of their transsexualism that may cause tension in interaction. The fact that they do not possess ovaries and that they have acquired the remainder of their female equipment "artificially" need not be known and perceived. Unless others know that the individual is a transsexual, there is no apparent reason for any stigma-generated tension in interaction. In this sense, the transsexual's stigma belongs to the category of blemishes of individual character inferred from a known record, not to the category of physical stigmas.

In view of the above, it is surprising that no transsexual has yet entirely passed, obliterating her past gender by vanishing from her old social world and emerging elsewhere. It is true that many transsexuals work at constructing a new identity for themselves, and there is a trend toward becoming a natural-born female through such achievements as new circles of friends, new jobs and the reformulation of past biographical events. However, at the time of our interviews, no transsexual could conceive of ever totally passing, that is, of ever minimizing her sex change operation to the point of seeing it as mere corrective surgery. True, many of the patients wished to label their conversion operation "corrective surgery," but none seemed to truly accept the implications of such a definition, as indicated by the fact that every one of them foresaw situations in which it would become necessary to reveal the "truth." Most of these hypothetical situations involved future boyfriends, husbands or children. Adelaide, for example, when asked to whom she would be most reluctant to disclose her conversion operation, replied: "To strangers. But you couldn't be fraudulent with your husband. As far as the children are concerned, I don't know . . . it would be up to my husband; maybe I'd tell them when they get older. . . ."

Other patients, when asked whether they ever voluntarily disclose their sex change to anyone, answered: "Only in business dealings, when I have to, like applying for credit. . . . I told Mike of course [boyfriend] . . . and my boss; that makes it easier, that way I have nothing to hide. . . ."

"In general," one added, "I'd rather say corrective surgery. I wouldn't mention what it was. . . . I'll definitely tell my husband, though, when I get married, and my children will know that I had corrective surgery. . . ."

Jane, it may be recalled, was a stripper who said: "I'd tell my husband. . . . I don't know about the children; if they were older and the kids at school were talking about it and one of my children came home and said 'Mom, the kids at school say you're not really my mom!' Well I would *have* to tell wouldn't I?"

But Sylvia, a housewife type and more eager to pass, had disagreed: "No, I'd never tell them," she insisted. "I'd move out of the state so no one knows."

To this Jane replied: "If they love you," she said, "it'll be alright anyway. . . ."

"That depends on the child," Sylvia said. "You can't be sure. . . . If I'd adopted very young children I would just move as far as possible so they'd never find out."

Most other transsexuals concurred that the sex change should be revealed to one's husband. One patient, operated upon only recently, said: "I wouldn't tell a date . . . but I think my husband should probably know. . . ."

Another transsexual was even more explicit: "If I ever got married my husband would have to know or else I couldn't live with him. It would only be fair to him and if he loved me enough it would be alright."

Thus, all transsexuals felt that sooner or later they would have to tell somebody, most likely their future husbands and possibly also their adoptive children. Total passing was not contemplated by any transsexual. In addition, there was a generally shared feeling as to why such voluntary disclosure to husband and children must take place, however painful and risky: this was because of the potentially much more terrible consequences of being found out! Jane, who was quoted above disagreeing with her friend about the issue of disclosure, specified why she felt that she had to tell her children. "The chances of them [the children] finding out are too great! You're better off telling them!"

Another subject's reply to the question about disclosure revealed the same anxiety. When asked whether she ever voluntarily reveals her gender identity, she said: "Yes, if I am going with somebody and I feel that I should tell rather than have him hear it from someone else."

Apparently each transsexual felt that in some situations her identity was — and was to remain — problematic and hence a source of tension. The prevailing view was that sex change is such an important — and in the eyes of normals — stigmatizing experience that the risk of being found out outweighs the cost of disclosing it voluntarily and risking rejection, at least in situations involving intimate others.

Even though transsexuals may tend more and more to pass with increasing time after their conversion operations (see Chapter 4), no transsexual had passed altogether, not even those who had undergone surgery as far back as two years ago. Most of the patients were not in an allout effort to hide their sex change. Rather, they had been interacting a great deal with others who knew, openly bearing the heavy identity of the transsexual. The motives for doing this were discussed earlier. They are nicely summarized by one stripper type, who said, when asked how many people knew: "I realize this sounds funny, I should be around more people who don't know, but I guess it's a fear right now, maybe because it's still too new to be around people who don't know. It's a feeling of adjusting you know. . . . I disclose it if someone really puts it on me, like if they find out from someone else and keep questioning me, then there is no point in me pretending and trying to lie."

Thus all transsexuals were faced with the problem of tension management, since all experienced situations in which their stigma was known.* How was the tension handled?

Methods of Tension Management

In extreme cases, patients simply had to remove themselves from a tense situation. For example, one transsexual explained her situation as follows: ". . . my former boss hated the idea of me being a transsexual so much I had to change jobs."

What other, less drastic, ways were used by transsexuals to handle the tension ensuing from the knowledge of their gender identity?

Goffman specified a number of tension management devices that any person with discredited stigma might employ. One way to handle stigma-generated social tension is to treat the stigma symbol(s) with levity, thereby minimizing its importance. Or else, the discredited stigma may be referred to in certain "in" or slangish terms even though one is in the presence of "out" people — for example a Negro calling himself "nigger" in white company or a homosexual joking about "queers" in heterosexual company. The shock value of such strategies may help to break the ice in strained encounters. A further method that may be employed in such situations, Goffman suggests, is the voluntary and advance disclosure of one's stigma.

Questions were constructed to specifically discover whether such methods operate among transsexuals. In addition, this group was found to handle stigma-generated tension in a number of other ways. Sometimes, simple withdrawal into the in-group was the preferred way of life. More interestingly, there were various psychological mechanisms whereby transsexuals *define* their

---

*However, one type of tension may not characterize transsexuals any more than natural-born females at this time. In a recent article (Kando, 1972), I argued that the amount of sex role strain currently experienced by women is high (thus leading to the women's liberation movement), while transsexuals and men experience less role strain in this area.

situation as suitably as possible. The patients often maintained that no matter how much tension they had to endure as a consequence of being feminized transsexuals, this was far less severe than it had been prior to surgery. Or, they were willing to acknowledge that they were operating under certain strains, but this was no different from any other gender. Finally, many transsexuals simply denied tension in interaction altogether.

To examine the possibilities suggested by Goffman, the following questions were asked:

1. Do you ever joke about your sex conversion operation with people who have not had such an operation?
2. Do you refer to those who have had a sex change operation in the same terms when you are with other transsexuals and when you are in the company of nontranssexuals?
   More generally, do you use different terms, a different vocabulary in the two types of situations?
3. Do you ever voluntarily disclose the fact that until recently you were a biological male and that you have had a conversion operation?
4. Who are you or would you be most reluctant to disclose your recent conversion operation to?

Levity

The majority of transsexuals did not admit to ever joking about their condition. One reaction shows perhaps why: "I don't take this as a joke," she replied indignantly when exposed to the question. "I can't answer that because I don't see it as a joke. It's a very serious part of my life. . . ."

I apologized and explained the purpose of the question, whereupon she added, somewhat cooled down: "Well, I'm a little sensitive about this because I have been made a joke of most of my life and I'm getting tired of it. Because people, they don't really know . . . I don't even know why you want to know a question like that. There is nothing really to joke about. We have individual personalities too, you know! We don't all think completely the same! We want to be seen as individuals, as women in the world!"

Such a reaction was typical of the sensitivity of many transsexuals regarding their state. However, several of them did express the ability to laugh at themselves and to share a certain gallows humor with one another and with homosexuals. Lisa, for example, said: "If someone cuts me down I just say, 'You're just jealous because they cut more of me than of you.' But I only joke with gay boys. I wouldn't talk that way to strangers."

Finally, joking was not always restricted to the "own." Sylvia, the shy girl who works as a secretary to a nun, told of a girlfriend in this context: "I sometimes joke about these things to her. She read this book that was written by someone who had had a sex change and the title of it was *I Was a Man* [laughs loudly] . . . We laughed a lot about that book because we thought it was such a ridiculous idea, 'I was a man'!"

A young married transsexual related similar experiences: "I have a few real good friends with whom I joke around quite a bit (about it)."

Such cases show that humor, while perhaps not used as a tension-reducing tool by transsexuals, does nevertheless serve a definite purpose in low-tension relationships.

Terminology

Little evidence can be reported on the use of slangish or "in" terms by transsexuals as a way of breaking the ice in strained interaction with normals. Most patients said that they dealt with everyone in more or less the same fashion, be it a transsexual, a homosexual or a heterosexual male or female. However, several transsexuals indicated that interaction with the out-group sometimes requires greater linguistic caution and the use of certain niceties and a facade which were unnecessary in the in-group. As one of them said: "When we are together [transsexuals], we sort of let our hair down, you know. You don't have to be on your guard. . . ."

Asked whether she uses different terms and vocabulary when in the presence of normals and when with other transsexuals, one respondent emphatically agreed: "Oh yes! I would say so!"

Another transsexual gave the following specific example: "I

wouldn't talk about my box with straights!'"

Thus, if anything, vocabulary seems to increase the social distance between the transsexual subculture and the dominant one.

Voluntary Stigma Disclosure

We have already seen that many feminized transsexuals find it necessary to reveal the nature of their operation to a variety of people. Most of them would at least tell their husband, children and intimate friends, as they feel that the risk of rejection resulting from stigma disclosure is preferable to the unbearable inner tension caused by what Adelaide called "fraudulence." As one of them said: "I told my boss. That makes it easier, that way I have nothing to hide."

Roberta's comments in this context show even more clearly that tension reduction is the explicit purpose of advance notification: "My family in Wisconsin doesn't know yet about the surgery. . . . I'm going to delay until I am up and around to go and visit them . . . let them know ahead of time of course."

Withdrawal, Neither into the Family nor into Gay Society

The simplest way for the transsexual to handle potential interaction tension is to avoid it. For example, we already saw that some of the patients changed jobs because their sex conversion was totally unacceptable to their former employers or colleagues. The general question is, of course: What ingroups or subcultures does the transsexual retreat into when escaping from the tensions that her stigma evokes in the society at large?

One haven may be provided by the family. Indeed some transsexuals now live under the shelter of their parental home. However, more typically the transsexual is either alienated from her family, or at best unwilling to seek refuge there. As Sally explained: "After the operation [my parents] disowned me, they don't want me to visit home. . . ."

Sylvia's case was similar: "My father doesn't want to have anything to do with me at all. . . . The family doesn't want me to come back. . . ."

Less dramatic but most typical are those transsexuals who have become so urban and nightlife-oriented that a return to their puritan rural homes of origin is not so much denied to them as simply inconceivable. As Renee, the stripper, said: "My family? I have no trouble from them. . . . Probably because of the type of life I lead, I don't mix my family with my friends . . . I've lived with my family all my life, but I could never go back. . . ."

Hence it would be unrealistic to expect the family to be a major refuge to the feminized transsexuals. An alternative haven is provided by the "own." This group consists not only of other feminized transsexuals, but also transvestites and homosexuals. There is, in Minneapolis and similarly in other cities, a subculture that consists of several dozens of feminized transsexuals, a larger number of transvestites who hope to receive surgery some day, and some homosexuals. The social life of this subculture centers around a number of gay bars and stripjoints, where several of the transvestites work as female impersonators and where some of the transsexuals, once surgically feminized, return to work in strip shows. This suggests that the most meaningful operational distinction between the transvestite and the transsexual is that the former has not had the surgery which the latter has.

While the clinical literature distinguishes between transvestism and transsexualism as two different pathologies — the transvestite finding sexual gratification in cross-dressing and the transsexual firmly believing that he is a member of the opposite sex (Benjamin, 1964, 1966; Driscoll, 1971; Stoller, 1968) — the present study notes their similarity. As I explored the transsexual's nightworld, I encountered a number of transvestites. Nearly every one of these was eager to undergo sex surgery. Transvestites who had not been selected for the University of Minnesota project were saving their money to finance a trip to Casablanca, where Dr. Burou performs sex change operations for approximately $2,000, or to Scandinavia, where they hoped to be helped by the Hamburger-Sturup team that had feminized Christine Jorgensen. In addition, we already saw that every transsexual in this study except Vanessa had been a transvestite prior to her operation. It is therefore important to realize that the borderline between transvestites and transsexuals is not sharp. The difference is one of degree, and becomes one of kind only with *feminized* transsexuals. There is a joint subculture, some of whose members have been surgically feminized – the transsexuals – and some of whom have not – the transvestites. Thus a central focus of the subculture was the discussion of and exchange of information about various medical and practical aspects of the sex change operation. The members know one another and frequent one another; there can be no doubt about the fact that they constitute an interconnected and to a certain extent cohesive social world – a subculture.

The group includes some homsexuals but it should be distinguished from the gay world: homosexuals involved in the transsexual-transvestite subculture are generally so by virtue of some personal relationship. For example, one frequently sees homosexual couples consisting of one "regular" homosexual and one transvestite. For such couples, the outcome of the surgical feminization of the transvestite is a heterosexual relationship, possibly even a formal marriage. This indicates that the transsexual-transvestite subculture ultimately believes in heterosexuality, not homosexuality. In this sense it sides with the culture at large and not with the gay world. As Garfinkel (1967) explains with reference to one transsexual, she agrees with the dominant society that one is either a normal male or a normal female, period. The transsexuals' negative attitudes toward homosexuality can be documented from the case material. One transsexual put it as follows: "I knew three homosexuals before my operation. I despised them. To me these affairs were not homosexual. They were very unsuccessful. They were one-sided. I played a passive role. I derived no pleasure from them. I felt I was a woman."

Another patient was even more adamant: "I hate homosexuals! I never wanted sex with them, only with straights. Homos are pigs. I don't tolerate them any more. I don't even want to read about them . . . homos get what they want!"

An attractive young stripper said: "I was never a homosexual in any form. I went to gay bars twice in my entire life. I was not accepted by gay society, nor did I wish to be."

Thus the gay world becomes one of the transsexual's negative reference groups. One could speculate about the amount of self-hate involved in such a reaction. In any event, transsexuals would clearly be the last to sympathize with the current liberalism embodied in such movements as gay liberation. The high degree of sexual conservatism noted among transsexuals earlier in this study (Chapter 2) makes sense in the present context.* It is understandable, therefore, that homosexuals are more marginally related to the world of the transsexuals than are transvestites.

There is, then, a distinct subculture consisting of transsexuals and transvestites. This group excludes homosexuals because its values are those of the culture at large and not those of the gay world. And it is clearly a group because its members know one another and interact with one another. It is into this group that transsexuals sometimes retreat to avoid some of the stigma-generated tension in the outside world.

While the transvestite-transsexual subculture provides a refuge to some transsexuals, many prefer to dissociate themselves from that world as well. In fact, to some patients it was not the gay world, but this transsexual subculture that functioned as a negative reference group. One patient expressed the following feelings: "I feel much more uncomfortable with transsexuals than with straights. . . . Most transsexuals here in Minneapolis are pigs. They have no moral standards. I can see why men categorize all of us as pigs."

Another transsexual evaluates her peers in a similar way: "I guess we are all exhibitionists after our operation, and this also builds self-confidence [the reference is to the nightclub jobs many patients take after their sex conversion]. But many of them live very unmoralistic lives, they go through a sexual binge afterwards. . . . My only binge was this dancing."

A third respondent's objections to frequenting other transsexuals are more practical: "As far as other transsexuals are concerned, we hinder each other, we don't do each other any

---

*Driscoll (1971) notes that there is a certain new militancy developing among some San Francisco transsexuals, embodied in an organization called COG (Correction of Gender). However, Driscoll's sample consisted of nonfeminized transsexuals and is therefore difficult to compare with ours. I expect that most transsexuals who undergo sex surgery would develop a high degree of sexual conservatism, particularly the passing housewife types, due to the tremendous investment made into conventional femininity.

good. We don't behave well en masse. . . ."

Thus, while some transsexuals prefer to go it alone, some choose the relatively secure world of the in-group as a protection against tension in the outside world.

Summary and Conclusion

The transsexual's interactions are characterized by at least two features: in some situations they are known to bear stigma, and in some they pass as natural females. While several transsexuals could ideally pass as natural-born females in most of their life situations, it was shown that they sometimes prefer to disclose their true condition and to manage the ensuing tension, rather than having to risk involuntary disclosure. Faking it still appears hazardous to most of them, particularly with intimate others, and passing attempts are often considered fraudulent. However, data indicate that in time, more transsexuals attempt to pass altogether, i.e. to claim natural femininity in all situations, including the sex act.

The self-imposed tension resulting from transsexuals' un-willingness to conceal their stigma is handled in a number of ways. Goffman had suggested that the discredited − those operating in situations where their stigma is known − may alleviate the stigma-generated tension by dismissing the stigma's importance through humor; by referring to it, and to oneself, in humorous, slangish and somewhat shocking terms so as to break the ice; or by announcing the stigma in advance of an encounter. These methods were found to operate among transsexuals. In addition, some transsexuals withdraw from stigma-generated tension into the in-group. This is a distinct subculture consisting of transsexuals and transvestites, but few homosexuals. Unlike the gay world, it firmly believes in heterosexuality and defines its own activities as heterosexual.

In addition to biographical reconstructions, transsexuals tamper with reality in other ways as well. There is a general tendency on their part, as perhaps among other stigmatized individuals, to define problems away. For example, all patients concurred that they operated now under much less tension than before the operation. Sylvia remembered how things had been before: "Well, evidently I appeared to people to be feminine, although I didn't realize it at the time . . . well I did too, but I wasn't trying to be feminine, if you understand. . . . People started noticing it more when I started high school I guess. . . ."

"Well, and how do you feel now?" I asked.

"How do you mean?"

"How has the transition affected you?"

"Well, it's just easier to live, when you walk down the street no one notices that you are unusual . . . this is a big thing in itself! Before, I felt like a woman and if I behaved like a woman it was noticeable and nonacceptable, whereas now it's acceptable. In fact a woman can behave in almost any way and it's acceptable, I mean respectable. There isn't as much emphasis put on how a woman acts as there is on how a man acts. A man must act slightly masculine. If a woman acts masculine, people don't notice it as much as they do if a man acts feminine."

In sum, one feature shared by many transsexuals was to consider their present condition less strenuous than their condition prior to the operation — it had been worse to be seen as an odd male than to be a feminized transsexual.

REFERENCES

Benjamin, Harry: Nature and management of transsexualism, with a report on 31 operated cases. Western Journal of Surgery, Obstetrics and Gynecology, 72:105-111, 1964.

——— The Transsexual Phenomenon. New York, The Julian Press, 1966.

Driscoll, James P.: Transsexuals. Transaction. Special Supplement. March-April, pp. 28-37, 66, 68; 1971.

Garfinkel, Harold: Studies in Ethnomethodology. Englewood Cliffs, N.J., Prentice Hall: 1967, pp. 116-185.

Goffman, Erving: Stigma: Notes on the Management of Spoiled Identity. Englewood Cliffs, N.J., Prentice Hall, 1963.

Kando, Thomas: Role Strain: A comparison of males, females and transsexuals. Journal of Marriage and the Family, August:459-464, 1972.

Stoller, Robert J: Sex and Gender: On the Development of Masculinity and Femininity. New York, Science House, 1968.

Chapter 6

TRANSSEXUALISM AS A SOCIOLOGICAL PHENOMENON

$\Big($ $\Big)$

IN the previous chapters, the various modes of postoperative adjustment among transsexuals have been examined and documented. The transsexual phenomenon may now be placed in the sociological perspective outlined at the outset of this book.

The study developed under at least the following six major influences: the approach has been primarily ethnographic-descriptive, rather than hypothesis testing; some of the methodological recommendations that have been followed may be termed phenomenological; basic to the approach has been the relativism that is the sociology of knowledge's subject matter; central to the approach has been symbolic interactionism's conception of man as an interpreter and society as an interpretive process; the study shares with the sociology of the absurd the assumption that conflict and meaninglessness are natural; finally, ethnomethodology was considered the most desirabale type of knowledge that could result from such a study of transsexuals.

On the other hand, two alternative focuses were consciously rejected: the etiological interpretation of transsexualism based on psychiatric and medical theories; and the test, by way of quantitative variable analysis, of articulations derived from the functionalist-role theoretical paradigm. In the next pages I explain the reasons for and the consequences of these theoretical-methodological choices.

Theoretical and Methodological Background of the Study

It should be stated at the outset that the reasons for

incorporating or rejecting various influences in the overall approach of this study all hang together. They basically center around the fact that a study of a novel phenomenon such as transsexualism is likely to benefit most from unstructured observation of as many facts as possible, unhampered by a priori theoretical restrictions. At the same time, a number of alternative approaches had to be considered. At the risk of some repetitions, I shall now attempt to deal briefly with each of these seriatim.

The Ethnographic Approach

In the first place, then, the study is essentially an ethnography of feminized transsexuals. The ethnographic tradition, although currently gaining adherents among sociologists, is older and more widespread among anthropologists.* This indicates that exploratory studies are better served by descriptive, unstructured methods designed to gain as much information as possible, rather than by structured operationalizations designed to test a limited number of a priori hypotheses. It was felt that a study of a novel population such as transsexuals should be exploratory and therefore ethnographic.

The ethnographic approach is, at its best, based on certain recommendations that are "phenomenological": the phenomenological method is an effort to "go to the things themselves." It consists of a number of mental reductions which enable the social scientist to approach a phenomenon free of any and all a priori cultural, sociological or personal theoretical suppositions — totally open-minded. The object of phenomenology is to understand a phenomenon in its own terms (Kruijer, 1959; Psathas, 1969; Wax, 1967). Objectivity, here, means the accurate rendering of the subject's subjectivity. In our study, transsexuals were approached somewhat in such a fashion, as ethnographers had approached certain non-Western societies in the past. Instead of

---

*It is well illustrated by such works as Bohannan, Paul: *The Tiv of Central Nigeria,* Malinowski, Bronislaw: *Argonauts of the Western Pacific; Coral Gardens and Their Magic,* Kluckhohn, Clyde, and Leighton, Dorothea: *The Navaho.* A good recent sociological ethnography is Spradley, James: *You Owe Yourself a Drunk,* New York, Little Brown, 1970.

applying existing social-scientific concepts and theories to the case
of the transsexual — for example functionalist sociological theory,
or psychoanalytic psychological theory — transsexuals were
viewed as part of a subculture that must be understood from
within, through empathetic understanding.

The Sociology of Knowledge

The fact that the relativistic outlook typical of the sociology of
knowledge has also influenced this study is related to what has just
been said. It was stated that transsexuals may best be viewed as
part of a subculture, and that phenomenological ethnography
attempts to understand any culture or subculture in its own terms.
An increasingly fundamental tenet in the social sciences is that all
social knowledge is related to its societal base. Anthropology has
taught us the lesson of cultural relativity. The sociology of
knowledge, inspired by Marx, teaches us that knowledge is
determined by the social position of its possessor. Current ethnic,
socioeconomic and sexual liberation movements question the
exclusive validity of traditional middle-class knowledge and values.
Forms of behavior that were until recently safely labeled criminal
or pathological are now viewed to be so only by virtue of
definitions imposed by the dominant power groups.* What was
viewed as mental illness is now viewed by some psychiatrists as
merely a different set of games (Szasz, 1961). In sum, we all seem
to be coming around to the realization that all behavior is
subjectively or subculturally meaningful, be it that of the paranoid
and homosexual (Lyman and Scott, 1970), the schizophrenic,†
the delinquent,** the ghetto dweller,†† or the transsexual. There

---

*George Bryan Vold, in his *Theoretical Criminology,* criticizes Sutherland's concept of
white collar crime precisely because it relativizes crime in this manner and thus, Vold
argues, renders the concept meaningless.
†The theoretical presentation of this point of view is found in Bateson, Gregory, et al.:
Toward a theory of schizophrenia. *Behavioral Science,* October 1956, pp. 251-264. A
fiction novel making the same point is Green, Hannah: *I Never Promised You a Rose
Garden.* New York, New American Library, 1964.
**The concept of delinquent subculture is relatively old. See for example Cohen, Albert
K.: *Delinquent Boys.* Glencoe, Ill., Free Press, 1955; Miller, Walter B.: Lower class
culture as a generating milieu of gang delinquency. *Journal of Social Issues, 14*(3): 5-19,
1958; and Bordua, David J.: Delinquent subcultures: Sociological interpretations of gang

-------->

seems to be a new sociology emerging which concerns itself primarily with the discovery of subjective and subcultural meanings.* This can only be accomplished by placing oneself into the subjects' own frame of meaning and thus discovering the theories and methods which they use to construct their social world. The transsexual's subculture, which also includes transvestites, female impersonators, some homosexuals and perhaps others, represents a distinct social position which produces a distinct world view and a set of theories and methods of operation.

Symbolic Interactionism

While the sociology of knowledge emphasizes the differences in the meanings that events acquire as a result of different (sub-) cultural interpretations, symbolic interactionism emphasizes that all human behavior is interpretive behavior and that all meaning is man-made. In Mead's well-known words: the meaning is in the response. Mead emphasized that man not only responds symbolically and interpretively to his environment, but also always responds to himself in such a fashion. Man is self-conscious, able to objectify himself as he objectifies others, always engaged in simultaneous dialogue with himself and with others. To paraphrase Cooley's looking-glass self: I know me, I know others, and I know how others know me.

Symbolic interactionism grasps well the behavior of a deviant minority such as transsexuals and their relationships to others, because its concepts allow for variability in the quality of communication and interaction. It conceives of interaction as a multiphased process in which the various phases rarely coincide

---

*While there may not be a new unified paradigm (if there were one, there would not be so much talk of crisis in the discipline), a variety of new sociological work seems to be converging toward such a "new sociology." The best example is Lyman and Scott (1970).

---

delinquency. *The Annals of the American Academy of Political and Social Science,* November 1961, pp. 119-136.

††For a humorous illustration of the relativity of cultural deprivation, see the *Dove Counterbalance Intelligence Test* developed by Watts social worker Adrian Dove (unpublished).

totally. It recognizes that social definitions, self-concepts and identities are not necessarily validated by others, that meanings are often not shared, that much interaction is devoted to the negotiation of problematic definitions, meanings and roles. Thus an important program suggested by symbolic interactionism is the discovery of the mechanisms whereby individuals and groups arrive at the minimum definitional consensus required to sustain relationships, and the mechanisms that sustain relationships in the face of lack of agreement. Indeed, many relationships are characterized by mutual understanding combined with rejection — empathy without sympathy.

Conflict

The inspiration which this study received from conflict sociology and from such related theoretical works as *A Sociology of the Absurd* is directly related to what has just been said. Because there is no inherent meaning in the world itself, conflict and absence of consensual definitions are natural. It is more logical to assume that man's natural state is, as described by Hobbes, a state of war of each against all, than it is to assume, with functionalist sociology, that social order is natural. Insofar as communication and societies exist, they are human productions and it is the sociologist's task to explain these unlikely phenomena, not to take them for granted. The existence of sustained relationships does not necessarily indicate the absence of dissent, hostility or mutual discreditation. A properly functioning social system does not necessarily imply the absence of conflict, rebellion and deviance. In fact, a certain permanent margin of deviance, and its open punishment, have been viewed as functional for the overall system because they maintain its normative boundaries and reinforce the collective conscience (Durkheim, 1958; Erikson, 1962). Therefore, while society may undergo normative liberalization with regard to certain areas of its culture, there will always be *some* forms of discredited behavior. While the specific behavior that is stigmatized may change from one historical period to another and while today's deviants may be tomorrow's normals, deviance and stigma per se remain.

Whatever, then, the specific nature of stigma may be, it remains an important factor in society. Stigma plays an important role in a vast number of relationships that are nevertheless sustained. Thus, an important task for sociology is to discover how relationships are sustained in the face of stigma, mutual discreditation and lack of consensual definitions of situation and identities. The relationships of transsexuals with others are, of course, a case in point.

Ethnomethodology

The final influence received by this study, that of ethnomethodology, is a direct consequence of the above. Since it was stated that individuals sustain relationships in the face of mutual discreditation, it follows that they must find methods to do so, i.e. methods to facilitate social action. Ethnomethodology is that branch of sociology which defines its task as the unmasking of the latent and tacit methods that make orderly and routine social action possible. In Garfinkel's words, ethnomethodology discovers the *members'* own methods of operation. Needless to add, ethnomethodology seems to pick up the heritage of phenomenological ethnography as discussed earlier.

The present study may be viewed as ethnomethodological in two ways, depending on who the "members" are. If a study of transsexuals produces only a better knowledge of *those members'* methods of operation, it remains an interesting vignette at best. In such a case we have a descriptive ethnography of a limited population, with little or no sociological generalizability. However, a second possibility is to *use* transsexuals as a tool for the unmasking of the latent theories and methods of the population at large. This possibility is suggested by the fact that a favorite method of Garfinkel's and his disciples is to expose routine behavior to disruptions and to the unexpected. Transsexuals most certainly present us with the unexpected: first, they have shattered one of the most fundamental tacit understandings that underlie the social order — the understanding the gender-identity is nonnegotiable. Having done this, they then undertook to equal or outdo natural-born females in a variety of sex roles. Thus transsexuals provide us with a laboratory for the ethnomethodological study of sex behavior in two ways: as a group of highly self-conscious and sex-conscious individuals who may be aware of aspects of sex behavior which the rest of us take for granted; and secondly, as a catalyst that reveals the normative background and texture against which "normals" enact routine sex behavior unwittingly.

While some sociologists* have alleged that this unmasking of the normative background of interaction is useless and destructive, it does seem useful in the area of sex norms, an area with perhaps more taboos, unspoken regulations and tacit understandings of obscure origin and doubtful use than any other part of our culture. While both rejection and acceptance of traditional norms remain possible once the ethnomethodological unmasking has taken place, the unmasking itself is a worthwhile undertaking, both from the standpoint of knowledge and as a possible souce of social change. It is to this process that transsexuals may make a significant contribution, as would other individuals for whom sex roles are problematic.

In the present study, only a few hitherto tacit understandings held by normals with regard to sex came to light as a result of exposure to transsexualism. One case in point is the discovery that each gender tends to use a different definition of sex, depending on which criterion will enable it to be exclusively classified in the proper category. An additional discovery that pertains not merely to transsexuals, but to all relationships between normals and sexual deviants, is the use of the psychiatric symbolic universe as a common grounds on which deviant sexuality is handled in such relationships. Furthermore, an examination of the transsexual's theories and world view, of which a sample will be presented shortly, is relevant not only to transsexualism, but also for purposes of comparison with other categories of individuals. Finally, insofar as a whole variety of stigma management devices have been documented and shown to exist among transsexuals, these methods may be generalizable to other stigmatized populations.

To this extent we did more than just report on transsexuals. In the last part of this chapter, some suggestions will be offered for

---

*See for example Gouldner's severe critique of Garfinkel's ethnomethodology (Gouldner, 1970).

further research on stigma management and toward a general theory of stigma. Of course, it may be argued that the documentation of a number of stigma management devices by transsexuals is not really ethnomethodology, since it does not break down the members' methods into fine logical categories. Nevertheless, while the internal structure of these methods is not clear, their observation and documentation among transsexuals may be helpful for a better understanding of stigma management.

The influences that have helped shape this study have been enumerated and discussed. In the last few pages, the following sociological approaches were dealt with: the ethnographic tradition, the phenomenological method, the sociology of knowledge, symbolic interactionism, the sociology of conflict and the "sociology of the absurd," and finally ethnomethodology. Of course, the relationships, the overlap and the mutuality among these traditions have not been clarified. For example, it can be argued, as Psathas did, that phenomenological ethnography and ethnomethodology constitute essentially the same enterprise. One thing seems to be clear at this point in the history of sociology: each of these traditions is located outside the functionalist paradigm of sociology. Thus, when the current chaotic conditions in our field — be they termed a scientific revolution (Kuhn, 1962) or a crisis in Western sociology (Gouldner, 1970) — begin to clear up and theoretical integration proceeds toward the formulation of a new paradigm, the approaches discussed in the preceeding pages may be expected to play a role.

Not only do the traditions underlying this study stand in antithesis to the structural-functional paradigm and its prevailing methodology, but they also differ from the classical psychiatric model. I shall now briefly deal with each of these two approaches, both having been considered but rejected as the study got under way.

Shortcomings of Alternative Approaches

The Medical Model

One alternative possibility, then, was to have followed in the footsteps of the medics and psychiatrists who have examined transsexualism, dealing mostly with the background history and etiology of the pathology. These experts have had access to extensive biographical and in-depth psychological data on their patients over long periods of time. Even so, their discussion dealing with the etiology of the condition and possible cure remain speculative. It is still not clear whether the pathology is organic or environmentally induced, how it develops, and how it may be cured. Our data, on the other hand, were collected only after the operations, over a short period of time, and no indirect psychological techniques were used to analyze the transsexuals. Hence the resulting material consists of a description of the subjects' current lives and state of mind. Their motives were recorded, but no attempt was made to explain transsexualism on the basis of background biographical information or projective personality inventories.

Classical Variable Analysis

A second possible approach would have been the deduction of formal hypotheses from the sociological paradigm and their test among transsexuals. Initially, that approach was followed. An attempt was made to use role theory as a deductive framework for the formulation of a number of propositions, which were then operationalized and tested through quantitative variable analysis. The independent variable was transsexualism, so that transsexuals had to be compared with nontranssexuals. The dependent variables were derived from role theory. However, only a number of commonsensical variables could be arrived at, for example role strain, role conflict, reference group conflict, marginality, and (in-)accuracy of role-taking. While the quantitative comparison of transsexuals with randomly selected control groups of males and females yielded some statistically significant differences (Chapter 2) to which we shall return in a moment, it soon became apparent that a sociological first such as the present study ought to be exploratory. It would have been a shame to utilize this novel population for the test of preconceived sociological hypotheses only, ignoring many interesting and unknown aspects of the transsexual's social life. Hence, as explained earlier, the study became an ethnography.

Blumer pointed out nearly two decades ago that conventional variable analysis limits the range of possible relevant questions that the sociologist may ask. What, precisely, would have been the limitations imposed by such a procedure in our case? Most conventional research deduces hypotheses from the prevailing paradigm, operationlaizes them and tests them. Standard sociological research consists of articulating the existing paradigm and testing these articulations. While it may be difficult to name that paradigm (it cannot be altogether equated with structural-functionalism), it is undoubtedly true, as Gouldner for example recently showed, that there *is* such a paradigm which still dominates sociology and which, in fact, is under increasing attack.

When using this paradigm as a point of departure, the sociologist studying, for example, deviant sexuality would probably test a number of hypotheses that predict the causes of successful social adjustment on the part of the deviants. He would probably begin articulating the paradigm in this area by elaborating some role-theoretical concepts, postulating first, for example, a correlation between adequate socialization into sex roles on the one hand, and adequate adjustment to the larger social system on the other. Then, this generalized prediction would be further specified with reference to limited populations and/or conditions, and these tentative specific answers to a basic sociological questions would then be tested.

The problem with this procedure is that, since the paradigm only allows for those articulations which the conceptual framework permits, therefore a wide variety of findings is totally beyond its vision. While earlier in the development of the current body of sociological knowledge this paradigm may have provided the necessary articulations to lead researchers in constructive research, an increasing number of sociologists now experience it as an obstacle to the open-minded approach to new phenomena, the possible discovery of new social processes and the creative formulation of new questions and new sociological interpretations of behavior. In the present case, for example, it was felt that the transsexual's social relationships, their success as women, what "success" in fact means, these and similar questions were best left open. There was little use for prestructured hypothetical answers to any question dealing with the transsexual's social relationships.

This, then, explains the absence in our study of a coherent theoretical model from which hypotheses would have been deduced and then tested. At the same time, theory was far from ignored: the central argument in this chapter has been that our study is not so much atheoretical as outside the realm of the current sociological paradigm. This, of course, is no longer a novelty in the current state of the discipline.

Areas Covered by the Study

Picking up the six theoretical-methodological strands that have been incorporated in our approach, it can now be shown that those traditions did suggest a number of specific phenomena that had to be attended to in the study. This has been a study of the relationships between a sexually deviant subculture and the dominant society, and attention went mostly to the following three areas: the definitions and theories held by transsexuals (with regard to sex), compared and contrasted with those held by the dominant middle-class society and by some other sexual deviants, for example homosexuals; some of the ways in which transsexuals and others arrive at some common understandings with regard to sex and gender; and, finally, some of the methods used by transsexuals to sustain relationships with others in the face of discreditation. These areas of focus were directly suggested by the theoretical sociology discussed earlier in this chapter.

The Transsexual's Outlook

The picture of the transsexual's theoretical world view that emerged was one in which sex and gender are the crucial variables. There are few forms of behavior that transsexuals do not see as somehow related, causally or otherwise, to their performer's gender. This emphasis on sex as the major independent variable in society is obviously related to the transsexual's life experiences and social position. She, alone in society, has been both male and female. She is an expert on sex and gender. Her expertise is based not only on the sex conversion, but also on years of research, learning, experimenting and experiencing. Her knowledge of the chemical, psychological and social aspects of sex and gender is great. It is based on preoccupation with the subject, extensive reading, experimentation with various hormonal drugs and different sex roles, consultation with other transsexuals and with psychologists, endocrinologists and other specialists, and finally attentive learning from the occupants of the desired status, i.e. natural females.

Many transsexuals do a great of early reading in the medical, endocrinological and psychological literature concerning sex and gender. Christine Jorgensen, Agnes (the transsexual studied by Garfinkel) and the respondents of the present study had often done extensive research in this area long before their sex operation. It is often on the basis of such reading that self-experimentation with hormonal drugs begins. As these events take place, the transsexual is sometimes seeing a psychiatrist, psychologist, doctor or counselor. Finally, being acquainted with the world of sexologists through the professional literature and through information obtained from counselors and from other transsexuals, she then tries to contact the proper medical agencies for the sex surgery. The postoperative lifestyle of the transsexual continues to contribute to her profound grasp of both male and female sex roles and psychology. As a nightclub performer, as a prostitute, as a new woman, even as a housewife, she is continuously exposed to new learning situations. All in all, transsexuals live in a world in which sex is of the utmost importance, and they are exceptionally knowledgeable about it. Their social knowledge and perspective are reflected in a number of definitional and theoretical views which put them at variance with other cultural groupings. Six examples from the study will now be recalled.

In the first place, the subjects were found to define sex and gender in different terms than most males and females. For the transsexual, nature loses its primacy over nurture. It is possible to be a true female in spite of the possession of a male body. In the universal hierarchy of things, psychology becomes as important as biology. Transsexuals are unwitting solipsists, and this enables them to define themselves unequivocally as females, both before and after the operation. All but the three youngest patients said, as we saw, that they had undergone sex surgery for social-psychological reasons rather than for sexual-biological ones. The dominant society of course does not view transsexuals as full-fledged women because it defines sex biologically, not psychologically. While neither transsexuals nor the dominant majority are inherently correct, as was convincingly shown by Benjamin (1966) who pointed out the multiplicity of biological, psychological and social criteria that can conceivably be used to define sex, we have, then, two essentially different definitions of sexual reality. Most of us know our gender and know what it is because we were born that way. Transsexuals, however, see this as a tautology, and they question it.

A second feature of the transsexual's perspective is that she sees American culture with regard to sex as a narrow monolithic normative system dominated by rigorous middle-class standards. Transsexuals were found to be significantly more sexually conservative than males and females. Many of them, particularly the housewife types, were engaged in an effort to gain access to this alleged core-culture, to gain what they conceive of as middle-class respectability, ultimately hoping to pass as natural-born females.

The extent to which our normative system is monolithic with regard to sex is debatable. Since there is much talk of a sexual revolution, it is at least possible to discern an alternative view of things, one that views American culture as pluralistic and tolerant of a wide variety of sex behavior and sex norms, with no necessary stigma attached to all but the dominant forms. There is at least a growing minority of individuals who no longer subscribe to traditional puritan sex values. Psychologists and councelors advocate permissiveness toward and experimentation with sex behavior; women, homosexuals and the counterculture militantly advocate normative changes; premarital sex and divorce are so common that to label them as stigmatizing is merely a matter of semantics; sex and procreation are more separable than ever. These and related trends are reflected in the media.*

It is from all those who have abandoned the traditional conception of sexual morality that the transsexuals differ. Unlike militant homophiles, enlightened therapists and liberated women, transsexuals endorse such traditional values as heterosexuality, domestic roles for women, the double standard of sexual morality, the traditional division of tasks and responsibilities, and the discreditation of deviant sexuality. Unlike various liberated groups, transsexuals are reactionary, moving back toward the core-culture rather than away from it. They are the Uncle Toms of the sexual revolution. With these individuals, the dialectic of social change comes full circle and the position of greatest deviance becomes that of the greatest conformity.†

The transsexual's firm belief in heterosexuality is such an illuminating case in point that it may be mentioned as a separate case highlighting her overall social perspective. It is precisely in order to normalize a former homosexual relationship that some transsexuals undergo sex change. Far from militantly advocating their rights as a deviant minority, transsexuals wish to *become* normal, heterosexual women. In this respect their perspective is at the sharpest variance with those experientially closest to them — homosexuals.

A fourth aspect of the transsexual's conception of social reality is her belief that women are more tolerant and more understanding than men, particularly with regard to acceptance of

---

*Therapy through sexual permissiveness is a racket avidly exploited by "doctors" in various disciplines, and whose respectable outlet is, for example, the local supermarket. A sample of the "medical" literature from which suburban housewives may select as they pass the paperback section of the run-of-the-mill supermarket: Bach, Dr. George: *The Intimate Enemy; How to Fight Fair in Love and Marriage;* Chesser, Dr. Eustace: *Love Without Fear;* Ebon, Martin: *Everywoman's Guide to Abortion;* Eichenlaub, Dr. John E.: *The Marriage Art* and *New Approaches to Sex in Marriage;* Hamilton, Dr. Eleanor: *Sex Before Marriage;* J: *The Sensuous Woman;* M: *The Sensuous Man;* Chartham, Robert: *The Sensuous Couple;* Reuben, Dr. David: *Everything You Always Wanted to Know About Sex . . . But Were Afraid to Ask* and *Any Woman Can! Love and Sexual Fullfillment for the Single, Widowed, Divorced . . . and Married;* Wood, Dr. Curtiss: *Sex Without Babies;* etc . . . etc . . . ad nauseam.

†On the comparative sexual conservatism of males, females and transsexuals, see Kando (1972c).

transsexuals themselves.* As we saw, this is an erroneous belief, no doubt based on the transsexual's former life experiences.

A fifth interpretation shared by most transsexuals and obviously rooted in their cross-sexual experience is that our society subjects men to greater role strain than women. However, this, too, was shown to be untrue, at least as measured by the operationalizations used in this study. Certainly when it comes to *sex* role strain, women experience greater dissatisfaction than men.† Feminized transsexuals are apparently a minority that experiences male roles as more burdensome than female roles.

Finally, and related to the first transsexual theoretical belief discussed above, since psychology prevails over nature, sex becomes achievable and negotiable. This is perhaps the most fundamental way in which the transsexual's world view differs from that of the rest of us. As Linton explained some time ago, sex has been a universal criterion of status ascription, precisely because of its firm roots in nature itself. While a pluralistic picture allowing a greater margin for *behavioral* deviance with regard to sex may be emerging in our society, this is not happening with regard to gender *identity*. Here, then, transsexuals are at variance with society at large, advocating a highly revolutionary and subversive point of view.

The Transsexual's Reality Negotiation

While the transsexual's perspective and social definitions put her at variance with other cultural groupings, particularly the dominant society in which she lives, she nevertheless sustains interaction with others, including members of that dominant society. Let us now examine the negotiation of common understandings that facilitate interaction between transsexuals and others.

The negotiation of social reality is determined by power, numbers, competence in advocacy and politico-cultural climate.

---

*On the various levels of tolerance toward transsexualism, and how males, females and transsexuals feel about this, see Kando (1972b).

†On the comparative amounts of sex role strain experienced by males, females and transsexuals, see Kando (1972a).

While it is difficult to pinpoint the "other party" with which the transsexual's reality negotiation is taking place, it may safely be assumed that compared to that party she is a pitiful minority. However, if we tentatively view the other party as consisting of the dominant majority and its culture, then a number of factors may be discerned that work to the transsexual's advantage.

When viewing reality negotiation between transsexuals and members of the dominant society, at least four things must be kept in mind: In the first place, the dominant culture with regard to sex has traditionally centered around a hard core of bourgeois, puritan norms (Ellis, 1961; Farber, 1966; Heise, 1967; Mead, 1949; Owen, 1962). Secondly, however, the sex mores of the dominant society are currently undergoing liberalization (Ellis, 1961; Kinsey, 1948; Seward and Williamson, 1970). Thirdly, the liberalization, when extreme, means that normative stability is replaced by crisis conditions under which sex and gender become truly problematic. Fourthly, our society is becoming psychiatrized so that sex and gender become the focus and concern of psychiatric treatment. These four characteristics all apply to the dominant, middle-class Americans that we think of as "normals" and with whom transsexuals must interact. Under these conditions, what shape does that interaction take?

In the first place, no matter how profound cultural change may be, one traditional belief is likely to be retained above all: the belief that one cannot change sex. At the same time, foremost among the transsexual's demands is to be accepted as a full-fledged female. In one fundamental way, then, the negotiation of the transsexual's identity will not result in definitional consensus. The transsexual's self-concept will remain unreciprocated.

The second feature of the dominant society mentioned above, however, works in the transsexual's favor: since liberalization of sex norms and sex behavior is so much a fact of modern life, transsexualism is now certainly more likely to be viewed with benevolent tolerance than in the past. Some may still experience transsexuals as threatening or disgusting, and indeed the phenomenon has at times evoked obscene reactions (Jorgensen, 1968). However, it is also possible that an increasing number of people view them as struggling, hopeful, sensitive women who have been unhappy in the past and evoke sympathy as they embark on a second try. If this response becomes prevalent, it will be in part the result of sexual liberalization.

In addition to the generally desirable sexual *liberation* of middle-class America, however, our society is also undergoing some elements of a sexual *crisis*. Attitudes toward sex are becoming ambiguous (Ellis, 1961); dominant parental and legal standards of sexual morality are at sharp variance with actual practises, be it in the area of homosexuality,* abortion,† fornication,** prostitution,†† or pornography;*** marital roles are experiencing strain and change (Williamson, 1970); the sexual identity crisis epitomized by transsexualism is, in fact, general (Josselyn, 1970).

How, then, can we fail to be intrigued by the transsexual's experience? It seems that she has a very significant story to tell. She has lived in our midst, experiencing a range of sex behavior covering modal forms such as marriage and procreation, minority forms such as prostitution, homosexuality and transvestism, and finally the very rare experience of the sex change itself. The impulse, therefore, is to hear her out on the full range of her sexual experiences. That the extremely rare transsexual phenomenon — less than three thousand feminized transsexuals in the United States at the time of this study — has received such wide media coverage and public attention, that transsexuals

---

*The Kinsey Report's estimate that one out of six white American males is more inclined to sexual activity with his own sex than with the other sex is now considered to be an underestimate (Kinsey, et al., 1948). Nevertheless, this country has yet to seriously look into the recommendations for legal reform made by the British Wolfenden Committee in 1956. In general, the prevailing negative attitudes toward homosexuality hardly need documentation. For a recent discussion of this, see Hoffman (1969).

†For example, California's estimated number of abortions went up from five thousand in 1968 to seventy thousand in 1970. Yet the legal fiction in this state is still that the procedure must be medically therapeutic, and a current swell in anti-abortion lobbying may result in stricter legislation.

**Fornication is prohibited in all but ten states and it calls for penalties ranging from a ten dollar fine in Rhode Island to a three-year prison term in Arizona (Slovenko, 1965).

††Although it is believed that the number of prostitutes has not changed recently (Esselstyn, 1968), the general policy remains one of informal regulation at best, ineffective attempts at repression at worst (Lemert, 1951).

***The issue is well dealt with by Ned Polsky who, in effect, asks about the nature of a society that brings forth both pornography and its condemnation (Polsky, 1967).

intrigue so many of us suggests that it represents more than a mere curiosity: To some extent it may *signal, or symbolize, the increasingly problematic nature of sex itself.*

The fourth feature of the dominant society discussed here, its psychiatrization, is directly related to what has just been said. As sex and gender become problematic, Americans are turning to the mental health professions for help. This is a windfall for transsexuals, for the increasing popularity of the psychiatric vocabulary finally leads the negotiators of the transsexual's reality to some common understandings: while transsexuals may never be accepted as full-fledged females, they are now at least viewed as human beings deserving of care, and not to be blamed for their condition. Thus, a consensual assessment of the situation is arrived at. All parties involved, including the population at large, psychiatrists and transsexuals themselves, internalize such medical motives as "biological causation" (Benjamin, 1966; Hamburger et al., 1953; Jorgensen, 1968), early childhood socialization (Stoller, 1968), or some other form of medico-psychiatric explanation. Thus everyone, including the transsexual, can view transsexuals as circumstantially and/or environmentally handicapped individuals, with no fault attached.

Stigma Management

Having outlined some of the factors involved in the negotiations between transsexuals and others, we must keep in mind that transsexuals remain a stigmatized minority, even though the stigma may not entail blame. To complete the discussion of the transsexual in society, therefore, we must now make some final observations about stigma management. Goffman's discussion of stigma shows that it may be essentially handled in two ways: it may be concealed, or it may be recognized. Needless, to say, face-to-face interaction does not permit the concealment of perceivable stigma. Only when stigma is merely a *matter of record* can it be thus handled. Transsexuals straddle the distinction between perceivable and merely "knowable" stigma, thus providing examples of both types of stigma management.

It was found that the patients do not inevitably opt for total passing, even if they could. More subtly than that, they choose to pass or not to pass depending on the situation and on the rewards of each alternative. The issue of passing is not posed and solved categorically. On some occasions, passing and the management of information are considered to be the most desirable course of action. In other situations, stigma disclosure and the management of tension are chosen as the most rewarding alternative. Each situation is appraised with one primary objective in mind: the presentation and the management of the most rewarding identity possible under given conditions. With this in mind, transsexuals possess a battery of methods for different contigencies, both of the passing and nonpassing variety (Chapter 4). There may, of course, be a tendency on the part of any individual to engage *mostly* in passing, or nonpassing: hence the various models of postoperative adjustment (Chapter 3).

From the point of view of the dominant members, stigma concealment may be the more desirable situation in terms of tensionless interaction. However, from the point of view of the stigmatized individual, concealment may not be assumed to be necessarily more advantageous than disclosure. As the financially successful strippers indicate, stigma disclosure can offer rewards that concealment does not provide. In general, whether stigma is revealed or concealed may depend on its nature, the amount of information that must be managed for its concealment, the rewards to be gained from concealment and the amount of tension likely to result from disclosure. Passing and stigma concealment are likely to be accompanied by negative attitudes toward one's original identity, dissociation from the "own" and a negative view of the stigma itself, in sum — Uncle Tomism; whereas stigma disclosure may be accompanied by greater militancy and a claim to be deserving of equal rights. We find among transsexuals a whole array of mechanisms resulting in a variety of forms of adaptation to the stigma and to society — forms ranging from conservative to militant, from hypocritical to crudely candid, from puritanic to promiscuous, from self-denying to opportunistic, from guilt-ridden to cynical.

General formulations may apply to a variety of stigmatized minorities besides transsexuals. Social minorities coexist with and within the dominant society and its culture. Their social relationships are successful in varying forms and degrees. Each stigmatized individual acts *as he or she knows best.* This is the main point. Here, we have tried to discover the meaning of sexual stigma.

REFERENCES

Benjamin, Harry: Nature and management of transsexualism, with a report on 31 operated cases. Western Journal of Surgery, Obstetrics and Gynecology, 72:105-111, 1964.

––– The Transsexual Phenomenon. New York, The Julian Press, 1966.

Blumer, Herbert: Sociological analysis and the variable. Am Sociol Rev, December:683-690, 1956.

Durkheim, Emile: The Rules of Sociological Method. Glencoe, Ill., Free Press, 1958.

Ellis, Albert: The Folklore of Sex. New York, Grove Press, 1961.

Erikson, Kai T.: Notes on the sociology of deviance. Social Problems, 9:307-314, 1962.

Esselstyn, T. C.: Prostitution in the United States. Annals of the American Academy of Political and Social Science, March:123-135, 1968.

Farber, Seymour M.: Challenge to Women. New York, Basic Books, 1966.

Garfinkel, Harold: Studies in Ethnomethodology. Englewood Cliffs, N.J., Prentice Hall, 1967.

Goffman, Erving: Stigma: Notes on the Management of Spoiled Identity, Englewood Cliffs, N.J., Prentice Hall, 1963.

Gouldner, Alvin W.: The Coming Crisis of Western Sociology. New York, Basic Books, 1970.

Hamburger, Christian, et al.: Transvestism: Hormonal, psychiatric and surgical treatment. JAMA, May 30:391-396, 1953.

Heise, David R.: Cultural patterning of sexual socialization. Am Sociol Rev, October:726-739, 1967.

Hoffman, Martin: Homosexual. Psychology Today, July 43-45, 70; 1969.

Kando, Thomas: Role strain: A comparison of males, females and transsexuals. Journal of Marriage and the Family, August:459-464, 1972a.

––– The projection of intolerance: A comparison of males, females and transsexuals. Journal of Sex Research, August:225-236, 1972b.

––– Males, females and transsexuals: A comparative study of sexual conservatism. Paper presented at the Pacific Sociological Association Meeting, Portland, Oregon, April, 1972c.

Josselyn, Irene M.: Sexual identity crises in the life cycle. In Seward, Georgene H., and Williamson, Robert C. (Eds.): Sex Roles in Changing Society. New York, Random House, 1970, pp. 67-92.

Kinsey, A. C., et al.: Sexual Behavior in the Human Male. Philadelphia, Saunders, 1948.

Kruijer, G. J.: Observeren en Redeneren. Meppel, Netherlands, J.A. Boom & Zn, 1959.

Kuhn, Thomas: The Structure of Scientific Revolutions. Chicago, The University of Chicago Press, 1962.

Lemert, Edwin M.: Social Pathology. New York, McGraw-Hill, 1951.

Linton, Ralph: The Study of Man: An Introduction. New York, Appleton-Century-Crofts, 1936.

Lyman, Stanford M., and Scott, Marvin B.: A Sociology of the Absurd. New York, Appleton-Century-Crofts, 1970.

Mead, George Herbert: In Morris, Charles W. (Ed.): Mind, Self and Society. Chicago, University of Chicago Press, 1962.

Mead, Margaret: Male and Female. New York, William Morrow and Co., 1949.

Owen, C.: Feminine roles and social mobility in weekly magazines. Social Research, November:283-296, 1962.

Polsky, Ned: Hustlers, Beats and Others. Chicago, Aldine Publishing Co., 1967.

Psathas, George: Ethnomethodology and phenomenology. Social Research, April:500-520, 1969.

Seward, George H., and Williamson, Robert C.: Sex Roles in Changing Society. New York, Random House, 1970.

Slovenko, Ralph: A panoramic view. Sexual behavior and the law. In Sexual Behavior and the Law. Springfield, Charles C Thomas, 1965.

Stoller, Robert J.: Sex and Gender: On the Development of Masculinity and Femininity. New York, Science House, 1968.

Szasz, Thomas S.: The Myth of Mental Illness. New York, Dell Publishing Co., 1961.

Wax, M. L.: On misunderstanding Verstehen: A reply to Abel. Sociol Soc Res, 51:323-333, 1967.

Williamson, Robert C.: Marriage roles, American styles. In Seward, George H., and Williamson, Robert C. (Eds.): Sex Roles in Changing Society. New York, Random House, 1970, pp. 150-176.

AUTHOR INDEX

153

SUBJECT INDEX

A

Abortion, 148
Accomplices, 107-108
Accounts, 112
Adam's apple, 68, 85
Advertising sex change for money, 47, 49, 55, 59, 104, 114 (*See also* Show business, Stripper type)
Age, 10, 12, 13, 14, 17, 20, 40, 46, 48, 54, 55, 59, 60, 68, 70, 87
Agnes, 34, 143
Alcohol, 65
Aspiring housewife, 59-67, 78, 82
  sexual conservatism, 60, 64, 65
  straight lifestyle, 60, 64
  tendency to pass, 83
  unsatisfactory artificial vagina, 78
  unsatisfactory physical appearance, 60, 78
Attitudes, 22-24, 29-31
  toward men and women, 41, 52-53, 145-146
  toward transsexualism, 29, 30, 52, 53, 76, 146

B

Background, 21, 48, 49, 55, 60, 62, 65, 68, 90, 91, 93, 112
Biographical reconstructions, 98, 110, 114 (*See also* Sad tales)
Birthplace, 20, 40, 48, 60, 91
Breasts (artificial), 6, 85

C

Career woman type, 67-77, 78, 82
  competitive attitude, 76-77
  intellectual, 77
  liberated, 75, 77
  physical appearance, 68

wealthy, 71
Castration, 6, 17
Children
  postoperative desire for, 28, 39, 41, 51, 52, 53, 67
  preoperative, 13, 68, 70, 71-72, 107
Coaching, 101-102
COG (Correction of Gender), 129
Compartmentalization of social circles, 93
Complexion, 13, 40, 55, 68, 85
Conflict sociology, 36, 132, 136-137
Covalescence, 11, 13, 49
Corrective surgery, 10, 11, 12, 42, 51, 56, 60, 66, 110
  euphemistic use of, 51, 52, 96, 108, 114, 120-121 (*See also* Surgical complications)
Cosmetic operation, 11, 49
Counterculture, 80, 144
Cross-dressing (*See* Transvestism)
Cultural definitions of masculinity-femininity, 22-24

D

Dating
  postoperative, 61
  preoperative, 50, 55, 66, 70, 74, 111, 112
Definition of the situation, 95 (*See also* Biographical reconstructions, Euphemisms)
Definition of sex and gender, 27-28, 31, 41, 53, 58, 63, 65, 138, 142, 143, 144
Denial of tension, 114, 116, 124, 130-131
Deviance, 36, 80, 136
  sexual, 39, 47, 138, 141, 142
Dilation, 49
Dissociation from "own", 39, 42, 98, 109-110, 116, 129, 150 (*See also*

Homosexuals)
Divorce, 10, 13, 20, 56, 68, 70, 71
Documentary interpretation, 34 (*See also* Ethnomethodology, Qualitative methods)
Double standard, 43, 58, 145
Drag queens, 90
Dress, 6, 40, 44, 55, 68, 119
Drugs, 7

E

Education, 20, 40, 48, 55-56, 60, 65, 68, 93
Electrolysis, 6
Empathy, 134, 136
Esquire, 44, 54
Estrogens, 6, 18 (*See also* Hormones)
Ethnography, 14, 32, 33, 132, 133-134, 139, 141 (*See also* Participant observation, Qualitative methods)
Ethnomethodology, 32, 33-35, 36, 132, 137-139
Etiology, 8, 18, 93-94, 111-114, 132, 140, 149
Euphemisms, 108
Exhibitionism, 17, 42, 78, 129

F

Family, 9, 40, 41, 42, 48, 49-50, 56, 60, 61, 66, 70, 72-73, 101-102, 106, 107, 112-113, 126, 127
role in sex conversion, 57, 72, 102
Female impersonators, 4, 11, 12, 43, 47, 48, 50, 56, 57, 58, 90, 104
Femininity
scores, 85
postoperative, 6, 10, 14, 26, 48, 50, 119-120
preoperative, 62, 72, 112
stereotypes, 43
(*See also* Masculinity, M-F tests)
Fornication laws, 148
Friends, 57, 63, 66, 74-75, 101
Functionalism, 33, 35, 132, 133, 136, 139

G

Gay liberation, 144-145

opposition to, 129
Gay society, 4, 8, 43, 50, 57, 109, 111, 127, 128
Gender, 137, 146
attributes, 21-22
definitions, 27-28
misidentification, 53, 56, 73, 86, 119-120
(*See also* Identity)
Gender Identity Committee, 6, 7
Geographical mobility, 42, 87, 102-103

H

Hair, 55, 60, 68
cranial, 68
facial, 6, 44, 69, 85, 86
(*See also* Complexion)
Heterosexuality
belief in, 128, 130, 145
postoperative, 6
preoperative, 70
Homosexuality, 3, 4, 8, 13, 28, 46, 50, 123, 134, 148
covert, 89, 94
denial of, 46, 50, 74-75, 110, 111, 128
preoperative, 43, 48, 74, 89, 110, 111
Homosexuals
hatred of, 28, 39, 43, 110, 128
(*See also* Dissociation from "own")
Hormones, 5, 13, 17, 143 (*See also* Estrogens)
Housewife type, 10, 14, 15, 25, 38-46, 77, 82
generally young, 39
sexual conservatism, 39, 41, 43
tendency to pass, 39, 83
values privacy, 44-45
(*See also* Marital domesticity, Marriage, Respectability, Sexual conservatism)
Husbands, 10, 41, 44

I

Identity, 95, 137, 146
conflict, 17, 94, 148
continuity, 77, 85, 99-100, 109
deviant, 50, 67, 78, 109, 111, 135

You Will Be Interested Also In These . . .

Henry E. Adams & Irving P. Unikel — ISSUES AND TRENDS IN BEHAVIOR THERAPY. 288 pp., 38 il., 14 tables, cloth $10.95, paper $7.95

Mala Betensky — SELF-DISCOVERY THROUGH SELF-EXPRESSION: Use of Art in Psychotherapy With Children and Adolescents. 384 pp., 222 il. (32 in full color), $13.95

Richard H. Blum — DECEIVERS AND DECEIVED: Observations on Confidence Men and Their Victims, Informants and Their Quarry, Political and Industrial Spies and Ordinary Citizens. 340 pp., 1 il., 5 tables, $14.25

Brian M. Davies, Bernard J. Carroll & Robert M. Mowbray — DEPRESSIVE ILLNESS: Some Research Studies. 368 pp., 17 il., 88 tables, $19.50

Joel Fischer — INTERPERSONAL HELPING: Emerging Approaches for Social Work Practice. 704 pp., 19 il., 12 tables, cloth $16.95, paper $9.95

Frank R. Freemon — SLEEP RESEARCH: A Critical Review. 220 pp., 17 il., 14 tables, $14.50

Robert Friedman — FAMILY ROOTS OF SCHOOL LEARNING AND BEHAVIOR DISORDERS. 360 pp., cloth $14.75, paper $9.50

Max Hammer — THE THEORY AND PRACTICE OF PSYCHOTHERAPY WITH SPECIFIC DISORDERS. 464 pp., $16.75

Roger D. Klein, Walter G. Hapkiewicz & Aubrey H. Roden — BEHAVIOR MODIFICATION IN EDUCATIONAL SETTINGS. 568 pp., 77 il., 27 tables, $14.95

Samuel H. Kraines & Eloise S. Thetford — HELP FOR THE DEPRESSED. 272 pp., 9 il., $8.25 paper

Arthur G. Nikelly — TECHNIQUES FOR BEHAVIOR CHANGE: Applications of Adlerian Theory. 2nd Ptg., 244 pp., $10.50

Jonas Robitscher - EUGENIC STERILIZATION. about 144 pp., 1 il., In Process

Edward M. Scott — AN ARENA FOR HAPPINESS. 144 pp., 2 il., $9.25

Julie A. Sherman — ON THE PSYCHOLOGY OF WOMEN: A Survey of Empirical Studies. 2nd Ptg., 320 pp., cloth $10.75, paper $6.75

Hirsch Lazaar Silverman — MARITAL THERAPY: Moral, Sociological and Psychological Factors. 576 pp. (6 3/4 x 9 3/4), 4 il., 4 tables, $24.75

Lois Timmins — UNDERSTANDING THROUGH COMMUNICATION: Structured Experiments in Self-Exploration. 336 pp., $11.75

Benjamin Wolstein — HUMAN PSYCHE IN PSYCHOANALYSIS: The Development of Three Models of Psychoanalytic Therapy. 192 pp., 1 table, $8.00

CHARLES C THOMAS • PUBLISHER • SPRINGFIELD • ILLINOIS

DATE DUE

OCT 8 '79	SEP 17 '79		
MAR 20 '80	APR 24 '80		
MAY 8 '80	MAY 15 '80		
AP 27 '82	APR 22 '82		
MR 12 '90	MAR 16 '90		
GAYLORD			PRINTED IN U.S.A.